This book is dedicated to the memory of Dexter, who recently crossed the Rainbow Bridge, and to Tilly, Molly, Millie, Charlie, Sophie, Candy, Chloe, Dinky, Sally and Bobby, Benji and Sophie #2 all at one time, members of our family, you will never be forgotten, and especially to Sasha, whose story was the first in this series and who inspired me to write all the stories that have followed.

And of course, to rescue dogs everywhere.

Our rescue family

Dexter, passed away, June 2019

DYLAN THE FLYING BEDLINGTON

BOOK 6 IN THE FAMILY OF RESCUE DOGS
SERIES

BRIAN L. PORTER

INTRODUCTION

Welcome to the 6th book in my Family of Rescuedogs Series. Dylan, The Flying Bedlington was originally planned to be the 5th book in the series, but was put back in the running order when we lost our beautiful boy, Dexter, and I decided it would be appropriate to commemorate his life by writing his story, so poor old Dylan had to wait.

Dylan has been with us longer than any of our other dogs, he's now fifteen, so he is very much the old man of the pack, not that it stops him from enjoying life to the full. As you'll soon discover as you read his story, he's quite incredible when you consider the setbacks he has faced in his old age, but I won't give too much away at this stage.

There have been quite a few faces entering and leaving our little family during the course of Dylan's life with us, some of them you will be aware of from my Facebook page, but some might be unfamiliar to you. Every one of them have in some way enriched our lives, and those who are no longer with us, will never be forgotten.

So let's get on with the story, and I hope you enjoy the tale of Dylan, The Flying Bedlington, but before we do, as the Bedlington terrier is not as well-known as some of the more popular breeds, I thought you might be interested to learn a little about the breed.

The Bedlington Terrier is a small breed, named after the mining town of Bedlington in North East England. They were originally bred to hunt vermin and have subsequently been used for dog racing, various dog sports, and competitive showing. They are distinctive for their 'lamb-like' appearance, but they are skilled hunters and have often been described as having 'the body of a lamb, with the heart of a lion'. Their fur is also hypoallergenic.

One man and his dog

They are also known as the Rothbury Terrier, after Lord Rothbury, a real enthusiast who promoted the breed extensively, in the late 19th century. Although the first Bedlington Club was formed in 1869, and the first breed classes were introduced at a show in Newcastle in 1879, the breed wasn't recognised by the Kennel Club until 1948.

They are confident and good natured and can be very stubborn and tend to like the sound of their own voices. Despite their diminutive size they like to be 'top dog' within a pack and therefore need patience in handling and training.

And now, let's move on the tale of Dylan, the Flying Bedlington.

Handsome Dylan

1

ONE MONTH B.D. (BEFORE DYLAN)

FOUR WEEKS before Dylan entered our lives, Juliet and I decided we'd like to add a new dog to our family. We already had Sophie and Candy, the two Dachshunds who had shared my life and been my best friends for several years after my previous marriage ended in divorce. Sophie was a beautiful long-haired, tan, (officially known as red), standard dachsie, and my vet described her as the biggest dachshund he'd ever seen. Candy was a black smooth-haired standard. They'd been together since they were pups, so had virtually spent their entire lives together. Of the two, Candy was the more playful, her favourite game involved me having to tie a balloon to a door handle, and she would spend hours bouncing and jumping up and down, bashing the balloon with her nose, tail wagging furiously. I should mention that Candy's tail, long and slim, was like a whip and when wagging at top speed, was quite painful if it caught you across the legs. I nicknamed her 'Miss Whiplash'. Sophie was more sedate, and preferred to play with a rubber bone, or similar chew toy.

They were very lovable and very loyal and faithful towards

me, and Juliet felt it would be nice to have a new four-legged friend she could call her own. So, one day in January, we took the children with us to visit our local dog sanctuary in the hope we might find a suitable dog, one that would get on with Sophie and Candy, of course.

The two dachsies had been four and five years old when I'd adopted them, from a previous owner who could no longer keep them following a divorce and it was clear to me from the start that they hadn't been socialised with other dogs, so they were very selective with whom they got along with. Candy had been diagnosed with diabetes at the age of nine and I'd had to learn to inject her with insulin twice a day, and she was on a special diet.

This was our first visit to the local sanctuary, though it would be far from the last. Juliet, my stepdaughters Rebecca and Victoria spent about half an hour looking at the dogs in the sanctuary. We kept going back to one particular little dog, a scruffy cross breed, who looked quite underweight, but had a cute and loving face and a straggly, waggy tail.

We made enquiries at the sanctuary office and learned something of the dog's history. Apparently, she'd been owned by an old gentleman who absolutely idolised her. Sadly, he developed a terminal illness, and before passing away, he asked his family to make sure his little dog, Tilly was looked after and cared for after he'd gone. Unfortunately, his son's idea of caring for Tilly entailed leaving the poor dog in the garden, not allowing her in the house and gradually she became thinner and thinner, until another family member saw the state she was in and made the son take her to the dog sanctuary, as it was obvious he didn't care about her and had no desire to fulfil his father's dying wish.

She'd been at the sanctuary for two weeks and though they'd been trying to build her up, she was still underweight and very skinny, but there was something about that little scruffy dog that attracted us to her, and when she was brought from her pen to the office to meet us, it was a case of love at first sight!

We decided there and then that we wanted Tilly and she seemed to feel the same about us, as she indicated by jumping up onto my lap and wagging her tail furiously. We made the appropriate arrangements for the adoption and agreed to collect her in two days, giving them time to bathe her for us and have their administer her first injections, part of the adoption package. They also included microchipping in the package, but because she was so skinny, it would probably be too painful to do the microchipping at that time and they asked us to bring her back in about a month, by which time she should have gained a few pounds in weight.

Everything went well with Tilly's adoption, she was such a friendly little dog that Sophie and Candy had no problem getting along with her, though unbeknown to Juliet and me, we had entered upon the first stage of our long-term devotion to rescue dogs.

Candy and Sophie

Tilly soon settled into our home and our lives and Sophie and Candy got along with her just fine. After she'd been with us for two weeks, I took her to the vet for her second vaccinations. We soon noticed that Tilly was a very active dog. She loved to run, she was a very fast runner too, and to investigate new things and new places. She delighted in playing with dog toys of any description and gradually, Sophie and Candy accepted her fully and would join in her games. We were happy with Tilly, and we looked forward to being able to return to the sanctuary to have her microchipped. Sure enough, after she'd been with us for a month, we could see she'd gained weight and so, as the weekend was just around the corner, we decided Saturday would be ideal to visit the sanctuary once again to have Tilly microchipped, which all went well, though the day didn't end up quite as we expected.

As usual, the two girls accompanied us, and we took Sophie with us, to keep Tilly company. Candy was left on guard duty at home. Of the two dachshunds, Candy was the one who, of the two, could do a good job as a guard dog. While Sophie would greet almost anybody with a wagging tail and a sloppy doggie kiss, Candy was more wary. If there was a knock on the door, she'd be the one to bark, to let us know we had a visitor. Her barking lasted only as long as it took for me to tell her to be quiet, and she'd then resume her passive mode. The barking would be enough to deter anyone who might try to break in while we were out.

The two dogs seemed to enjoy being together in the back of our Mondeo estate car and as I looked in my rear-view mirror, I could clearly see two heads, up at the windows, watching the passing scenery.

On arriving at the sanctuary, we left Sophie in the car, as visitors were requested not to bring their own dogs into the grounds for health and safety reasons. That was okay, as it was a sunny, but not particularly warm winter's morning and I left the rear passenger windows open enough to allow a good passage of air to permeate the car. We weren't planning on being long getting Tilly's microchip implanted.

Victoria, Tilly and Me

2

A BLUE BEDLINGTON

AS IT DIDN'T REQUIRE all four of us to be present in the office while Tilly was being microchipped, I stayed with her while Juliet and the girls went to have a look around the sanctuary. Tilly was very well behaved, and the microchip was soon implanted just behind her neck, though she did squeal a bit, so she must have felt some pain as the chip went in. However, the pain was soon forgotten as Jennie rewarded her with a nice tasty beef treat.

As Tilly and I walked out of the office into the beautifully planted courtyard of the sanctuary, Juliet and the girls came running up to meet me, (the girls ran, Juliet walked fast).

"Brian, you've got to come and see this dog," Victoria almost shouted to me.

"What dog is this, then?" I replied.

"Seriously," Juliet joined in, "she's right. You know you've always said you wanted a Bedlington Terrier? There's lovely little one over there." She pointed towards a pen over the far side of the courtyard.

I was intrigued and followed the three of them across the courtyard to a pen where the Bedlington was being kept, Sure enough, it contained a small grey Bedlington Terrier, officially called a blue. The poor dog looked terrified, and as we stood looking at him, the poor thing just cowered away from us. We spoke to the dog softly and calmly, trying to give him some reassurance. Tilly stood wagging her tail, obviously being friendly towards the dog,

"Okay, let's go and find out about him," I said, leading the family back to the office, with Tilly in tow.

Jennie was surprised to see Tilly and I back so soon and thought there might be something wrong. I soon made her aware of our interest in the little Bedlington, and she told us the dog had only arrived at the sanctuary that very morning.

"He was left tied to the gates, and we found him when we arrived for work," she told us. "There was a short letter, in an envelope, pinned to his collar. The letter was anonymous and the gist of it was that whoever had left him at the gates, had somehow removed him from an abusive home and couldn't take the risk of being identified."

"Sounds very fishy to me," I said.

"We often get cases like this," Jennie told us. "Oh, the letter also said his name is Dylan, and he's very nervous of people."

I looked at Juliet, who without a word, gave me a barely susceptible nod, and I said,

"Can we take him for a walk with Tilly and Sophie? She's waiting in the car."

Jennie immediately agreed and called one of the staff to take us to fetch Dylan. The sanctuary has a large field adjoining it where it's possible to walk prospective adoptees to see how they get on with interested owners. The lady came and with a lead in her hand, she opened Dylan's enclosure and as soon as the little dog saw the lead, he literally threw himself backwards, colliding with the mesh at the rear of the pen.

"He's terrified of the lead," she said. "It's obvious the poor boy has been beaten or whipped with a lead or a rope of some kind, in the past."

"Poor little fella," I said. "Do you have any idea how old he is?"

"The letter said he's eleven months old."

"That's very specific," Juliet commented.

"We think whoever brought him here was a family member who didn't like seeing the way he was being treated," the lady told us.

"That's terrible," I said, as the lady next went down on her knees and spoke very softly to the traumatised dog. Gradually, she was able to get close enough to Dylan to be able to slip the rope lead over his head, and she led him out to meet us.

At that moment, I was very glad we had Tilly with us. She seemed to sense his pain and mental turmoil, and she just kept wagging her tail at him and before we knew it, she was standing side by side with him.

"Good girl, Tilly," I told her and reached out to take the lead from the lady's hand. Dylan immediately reacted badly and tried to jump away from me.

"Let me try," Juliet said and after a minute of trying, he accepted her as she led him across the courtyard towards the little gate that exited onto the path to the car park. I held Tilly who wanted to lead the way, and so our little procession arrived at the Mondeo and Sophie joined us as we walked to the field. She amazed me by seeming to accept Dylan right away. We spent around half an hour with Dylan slowly learning to accept our dogs, and us, though he remained very scared of me at first, which lessened a little towards the end of our time in the field.

What really surprised us was that Sophie got along great with Dylan. Maybe dogs have an inner sense that helps them identify when another dog has suffered physical or psychological trauma.

Tilly, Sophie and Dylan meet for the first time

We had Jennie's permission to take Sophie onto the premises when we took Dylan back, and after we'd handed him back to the staff member who'd taken him out for us. Once we were all in the office once more and Jennie had spent a couple of minutes making a fuss of Sophie, who she thought was absolutely gorgeous, I turned to her and announced,

"We'll take him."

"Are you sure? We hardly know anything about him, and you've seen the state of him."

"We're sure," I was adamant. "He's obviously traumatised, and he seems to be afraid of men in particular, but we're willing to take him and help heal his psychological wounds."

"Well, he'll be a lot better off with you and your dogs for

company than he was in his previous home," Jennie said as she reached for the paperwork that would make Dylan legally ours. We would have to go out and buy him some essentials: a bed, feeding bowl, new toys etc. so we arranged to collect him on Monday, which was the earliest Jennie could get him to their vet for his vaccinations, and then she'd microchip him before we arrived to collect him.

Dylan with Juliet, on the sanctuary field, pre-adoption

We reluctantly said a temporary goodbye to Dylan as one of the sanctuary staff took him back to his enclosure. We felt good though, knowing any other interested partied would be met with the news that Dylan had already been adopted, and was merely awaiting collection.

During the drive home, Juliet voiced her one concern over Dylan's introduction to the family.

"What if Candy doesn't like him?"

It was a logical question and one which in all honesty, I didn't have the answer to, not yet, so I speculated instead.

"I'm pretty sure that once they meet, Candy will see how well Sophie and Tilly are getting along with him, that should make for an easy introduction. I can't see Candy being nasty to him once she sees he's already accepted by Sophie, especially."

"I suppose you're right," she agreed, and I hoped that what I'd just said would prove to be correct. For now, though, we arrived home and Candy was of course pleased to see us but then she must have picked up Dylan's scent on our hands and clothes and also on Tilly and Sophie. She spent a long time sniffing around every one of us and I remember thinking that she'd have no problem recognising Dylan when he walked into the house on Monday.

For now, all that remained was the final preparation for Dylan's arrival, which I took care of on Sunday morning, buying him a nice new bed, with a warn, soft mattress, a really lovely new collar and lead and a few assorted dog toys, and we were ready for him. Somehow, we got through the day, and bedtime approached, with the girls asking if they could take the day off school so they could go with me to collect Dylan the following day. I think you can probably guess what my answer was to their plaintive pleas.

Monday dawned, and we went through our normal morning routine, and the girls reluctantly headed off to school. After walking the dogs there wasn't much we could do until the time came to go and pick up our new doggie addition to the family. At the appropriate time, Juliet and I left Tilly, Sophie and Candy at home and made our way to the sanctuary.

We decided we'd be well advised to both go to collect Dylan due to his apparent dislike, or fear of men. Once there, it didn't take long to deal with the necessary adoption paperwork and in what seemed like no time at all, Dylan was legally ours. My lifetime ambition to own a Bedlington Terrier was fulfilled.

Instead of putting him in the back of the estate car for the journey to our home, again due to his nervousness, Juliet instead decided to have him in the front of the car, on her knee, which worked a treat. Sitting up on her lap, he appeared enthralled as he looked out of the window as we travelled along, obviously enjoying the various sights of the countryside. Juliet also noticed what a perfect 'sit' he adopted on her lap, straight-backed and erect.

"He looks really proud and happy," she commented as I concentrated on driving.

"Perhaps he already feels that we mean him no harm, and is enjoying the attention you're paying him," I replied.

She had barely stopped stroking him and talking quietly to him from the moment we'd set off. The journey home, almost half an hour in real time, seemed to fly past and in what felt like no time at all, we were home, our precious canine cargo still sitting proudly on Juliet's lap.

As we alighted from the car, Juliet passed Dylan's lead to me and although he followed me through the front gate, I could sense that he wasn't entirely comfortable with me, as he kept turning his head, as though making sure Juliet was closely following us.

Once we passed through the side gate that led to the back garden, we let Dylan off the lead and opened the back door, to be greeted by the three dogs, that were eagerly awaiting our return.

When they saw Dylan, Tilly and Sophie, who already knew him a little, greeted him like an old friend, though Candy wasn't at all sure of this strange-looking newcomer who'd suddenly appeared in 'her' garden.

For those who are unfamiliar with the breed, the Bedlington Terrier has a unique appearance, very much resembling a sheep! Appearances can be deceptive, however. In some circles the Bedlington is known as the dog with 'the body of a sheep and the heart of a lion'.

They were originally bred in the north-east of England as hunting dogs and were extensively used by gypsies in particular for hunting rabbits, hares and other small to medium sized prey. They were incredibly fast, and some travelling folk would make their way down south and pit their dogs against the gentry's greyhounds in races. Of course, the well-heeled members of the upper classes couldn't imagine that these scruffy terriers, (they looked very different in those days) could outrun their sleek pedigree greyhounds. Unfortunately for them, the Bedlington Terrier was built for speed and over a straight course of perhaps half a mile, they surprised everyone, apart from their owners, by outstripping the greyhounds on many occasions, thus leaving the rich and wealthy a little poorer.

Over the years, the Bedlington was bred selectively until we arrived at today's sheep-like appearance. There are still two distinct varieties however, the show Bedlington and the working variety, which tends to retain more of the look of the original.

Dylan looked nothing like a Bedlington to be truthful. If you didn't know the breed, you'd have struggled to identify him. Luckily, one look had told me what he was, and I was delighted to have him here in my home. The following photo shows you the transformation from when we first adopted Dylan (left), to the modern-day version, (right).

The changing face of Dylan

Candy soon came to accept Dylan, and the four dogs all got on well together. The important thing for us, once we knew they all got along, was dealing with Dylan's nervous disposition, most importantly, his fear of men, and me in particular!

3

PTSD

DYLAN'S first few weeks with us were quite a trial, for him and for us. We quickly realised that our most important job was trying to cure him of his fear of men. It was like trying to cure a battle-scarred soldier of Post-Traumatic Stress Disorder, (PTSD). He'd obviously been so ill-treated in his early life (he was only a year old), that it wasn't going to be an easy task.

He was perfectly happy playing in the garden with the other dogs, particularly with Tilly, and would cheerfully go for a walk with Juliet and either of the girls, but although he'd walk with me, he always appeared hunched up and fearful, as if he was afraid of being hit or kicked at any time.

I was determined to help him get over his fear, and after reading as much as I could on the subject, I realised that the most important thing I needed to do was to show Dylan that I loved him and wouldn't hurt him. That was easier said than done.

He seemed to know some basic commands, such as 'sit', or 'come here', but anything else was going to be a struggle if I couldn't gain his trust. I'd read that some form of interaction was one way of breaking down some of the barriers, so one day, while shopping, I bought a couple of identical pale blue teddy bears, just the right size for a dog like Dylan to play with, or cuddle up to.

Dylan, Tilly, and teddy bear

Hooray! The teddy bears were a success. As he mostly played with Tilly, I took the two of them into the back garden and stood holding the two teddy bears in my hands, so they could both clearly see them. First of all, I called Tilly who came to me straight away. I gave her a teddy bear, which she quickly accepted with her tail furiously wagging, and happily ran around the garden with it, shaking it in her mouth in typical terrier fashion. Next, I called Dylan, holding the teddy bear at arm's length, in a non-threatening stance. I called him a couple of times and he hesitatingly began to approach me. When he got within a couple of yards of me, I quietly praised him for being a good boy and gently placed the teddy bear on the grass at my feet and took a couple of paces back, never taking my eyes off him.

Much to my surprise, he crept closer, and then, when he

got within range, he picked the teddy up and ran to join Tilly, who was already having fun, tossing hers around and chasing it. It wasn't long before one of the teddy bears was discarded and the two of them indulged in a game of tug-of-war with the other one. Remarkably, the teddy bear would go on to survive many weeks of being used as a tug toy, after which the second one was ready in reserve.

Gradually, Dylan seemed to accept me as being a regular presence in his life. The real clincher in terms of gaining his confidence was much more basic. At every opportunity, I would get down on the floor and softly encourage Dylan to lie with me, or if he was already lying in an appropriate position, I'd slowly move to lie near him. At first, I did nothing more than lie quietly near him, gradually getting closer as the days passed. Then, when I felt he was used to me being there, I'd start to talk to him, just simple things like 'good boy, Dylan' or anything that came into my head. The words didn't matter. It was the tone of my voice that was important and gradually the bond of trust was growing.

One day, after about two weeks of lying on the floor with him, I tentatively reached my hand out and tried stroking him, just for a second or two. Amazingly, he didn't jump up and run away. He let me stroke him for a few seconds and from then the trust seemed to grow with each passing day.

He'd allow me to walk him, or play with him in the garden, and though there was still a little nervousness about him, Dylan was growing more confident and trusting. Over the following months we all saw this growth in his confidence, though he'd still jump at loud noises and occasionally would even shy away from his lead if it swung too close to him before being clipped to his collar. The memories of what happened to him in his puppyhood must have been so deeply imprinted in his brain that even now, after 14 years with us, he still retains that occasional 'jumpiness' around his lead. We shudder to think how many times he must have been whipped and beaten with a lead or something similar in his early days. How any human being could do such a thing to a young puppy, just amazes and appals me.

The rest of Dylan's first year with us passed in a whirlwind as he and Tilly grew closer and Sophie and Candy continued to do their own thing, as dachshunds do, not wanting to socialise too much with the young interlopers in the house. After all, they were here first, weren't they?

There was another addition to our growing pack late in the summer. The sanctuary where we'd found Tilly and Dylan held its annual 'Fun Dog Show' and we went along to see what such an event was like, never having been to one before. The girls had wanted to enter Tilly and Dylan into some of the fun groups, but Dylan could still be a little nervous, so we just entered Tilly into the *Best Rescue Bitch* category. We were pleased when she came third and was presented with a rosette. Later, as I was looking around the various stalls, Juliet and the girls disappeared, saying they were going to have a look around the dogs in the sanctuary. I'm sure you can guess what comes next. You're right of course and a week later we were joined by Charlie, a sort of black Cairn Terrier, if such a thing exists. Our little Scotsman was a real cheeky chappie but could be a grumpy little thing if anyone or anything upset him. Together with Tilly and Dylan, we now had a trio of small terriers who did most things together. Charlie was a very obedient, well-trained dog who needed little from us in the way of behavioural training. In other words, he was an extremely easy dog to assimilate into our family.

With Tilly and Charlie by his side, Dylan really grew in confidence and eventually we felt that he'd got over the worst of the PTSD and was really beginning to enjoy life as he should be doing.

Charlie

All was going well for our growing family, but unfortunately, sadness was lurking just a few months down the line. More of that in the next chapter.

4

SADNESS COMES IN DIFFERENT FORMS

AS THIS IS Dylan's story, I decided not to dwell on some of the sad events that overtook some of the other dogs who featured in his tale. I must, however, mention the unfortunate times that befell us during the winter following his arrival.

It was almost springtime, but still very cold when we rose one morning and quickly noticed that little Candy wasn't well. She wasn't walking very well and when she went out into the back garden, she almost collapsed. As I previously mentioned, she was diabetic, and I assumed her problem was related to the diabetes. As soon as they opened, I called the vet, who told me to take her as soon as possible.

On our arrival we were seen immediately, and after a long examination, Candy's vet informed that, sadly, her organs had shut down. Put simply, my beautiful little balloon chasing Miss Whiplash was dying and there was nothing that could be done to help her. The vet told me that thirteen was a pretty good age for a diabetic dachshund, but that didn't stop me feeling that somehow, I'd failed my little dachsie.

I was left with no choice. I agreed to let the vet send Candy across the Rainbow Bridge, and a few minutes later, after I'd had time to say a very tearful goodbye and give her lots of loving hugs and kisses, Candy left this world and ascended to doggie heaven. I drove home in tears; together with Sophie, Candy had been my joint best friend, seeing me through the bad times after my divorce, and had lovingly accepted Juliet into my life.

Juliet was of course, upset at the loss of my little girl, and over the following weeks it became obvious that Sophie was really missing her too. After all, she and Candy had been together almost all their lives, and poor Sophie was now faced with a life without her best friend. As the year wore on, it became obvious that Sophie was extremely depressed. She spent most of her time in the back garden, just sitting, watching the world go by. She'd watch the birds coming and going, feeding at the bird table and she seemed to enjoy just basking in the sunshine on warmer days.

Juliet and I could tell she was pining for Candy, and there seemed little we do to help her. Almost inevitably, a few days after Christmas, Sophie appeared to be having trouble getting out of bed. I had to help her and managed to assist her out into the back garden. It was like a case of déjà vu, as she wobbled and staggered along trying to go to the toilet. My heart was in my mouth as I made a phone call to the vet, who once again told me to take Sophie in right away. I could hardly believe it when the vet informed me that, like Candy, Sophie's organs were shutting down. At the age of fifteen, my gorgeous Sophie had literally pined herself to death, so much had she missed her lifetime friend.

I had to go through the terrible experience of saying a final goodbye to her. This time was even harder, because after the vet had given her the injection and confirmed she'd passed away, I saw her eyes were just as they were when I gave her that last cuddle, still open as though she was staring right into my soul. The vet left me with her for a few minutes. I found it very difficult to stem the tears, but eventually, I managed to calm down, but once again faced drive home with tears in my eyes.

Juliet felt terrible for me. She knew how much Sophie and Candy had meant to me, as I'm sure most dog lovers will understand. When your dogs are your only companions after a life trauma, losing them is one of the most upsetting and traumatic things you can face.

It would take me a long time to get over the loss of Sophie and Candy, but little Tilly seemed to sense my pain and before I knew it, she'd become 'my' dog, attached herself to me and followed me everywhere.

Soon after, Juliet, in an effort to cheer me up I think, suggested another visit to the dog sanctuary. She was right of course. Seeing all those dogs in need of loving, caring homes upset me at first, as it always did, but seeing the wagging tails as they reacted to visitors, hoping to find a new family always brought a smile to my face. Dogs are so resilient. As we looked around the sanctuary, we came across an enclosure which surprised us. Instead of a mature, grown up dog, we saw a litter of six puppies!

Five of them were an assortment of black, and black and white collie crosses, and strangely, the sixth pup was a brown, shaggy-haired little thing, that we instantly fell in love with. A couple of weeks later, that shaggy dog, now named Millie, was on Juliet's lap in our car, as we drove her to her new home, where she quickly settled in with the family and with Tilly, Dylan and Charlie.

'The Fab Four' – Millie, Tilly, Charlie & Dylan

It was soon after we'd adopted Millie that we met Brian, the canine behaviourist with whom I'd eventually develop a great relationship and learn a lot from. It was an accidental meeting as we walked our dogs in the woods one Sunday afternoon. He was walking his own dogs, and when Tilly and Dylan barked loudly at his two collies, he stopped and asked us if our dogs always reacted in that way to other dogs. To cut a long story short, he introduced himself, gave us his card, and invited us to attend his next training session, which luckily was being held not far from our home.

So began a long and fruitful relationship that would help us, and our dogs tremendously, and eventually see Tilly become an expert on the dog agility course, and then go on to train as a search and rescue dog. It was through Brian's training that we realised Tilly's problem. She was super intelligent and needed more of a psychological challenge than she was so far being faced with. Once the training began, the barking gradually lessened until it disappeared altogether.

Thanks to the training sessions, we suddenly found our

home was a little more peaceful and our dogs definitely better behaved. As Millie grew into an adult dog, it became obvious that she, like Tilly, had a talent for search and rescue work, and when she was two years old, one of the girls who worked for Brian and also for the local volunteer search and rescue team, approached us one day with a request.

From watching Millie tackling the various search and rescue exercises during training classes, she was convinced that Millie would make a perfect member of the search and rescue team. In order to do that, however, Millie would need to live with her handler and take part in regular exercises and simulations. In short, Millie would have to leave us and live with Lynn, the girl concerned, and she was asking if we would be prepared to sell her.

Juliet and I were in a quandary. We loved Millie very much, but we also knew how much she loved doing the search and rescue exercises at the dog training classes. Would it be fair to stop her from doing something she obviously loved doing, and was good at and which would benefit people in general? In the end, we decided we wouldn't sell her, but would allow her to be part of the search and rescue team, donated by us. Lynn was delighted and thanked us profusely. Millie trotted off with her quite happily, with her tail held high, wagging for all it was worth, when Lynn came to our house to collect her.

Lynn provided us with regular progress reports, and we were happy to know Millie was making good progress and was well on her way to becoming an official search dog. That was, until the day we received a tearful phone call from Lynn to tell us that Millie, while getting out of the car, had suddenly run out into the road, and been hit by another passing car. She'd died instantly. What could I say? Both Juliet and I were extremely upset, and felt guilty at having allowed Millie to go to join the rescue team, but then we realised that accidents happen and that Millie had been living a great life, doing the things she enjoyed the most, and there was nothing anyone could have done to predict she'd run into the road like that. We couldn't turn the clock back, and had to accept that poor Millie was gone, but she wouldn't be forgotten.

5

DYLAN THE VILLAIN

NOW THAT DYLAN was settled in at home, his bad memories of his puppy days mostly cast aside, as far as we knew, we concentrated on ensuring that his life, and those of our little rescue family, were as happy and full of love as possible.

Our regular visits to the training sessions definitely helped, as the classes exposed Dylan to a variety of dogs and owners in a controlled and safe environment. Our pack had grown to four once more with the arrival of Molly, a West Highland White Terrier, who was given to us by her owner who didn't feel capable of looking after her anymore. Molly was an older dog, fully house trained and didn't need much in the way of obedience training, but our reason for attending the training sessions wasn't so much for obedience training as it was for the dogs to have some fun, engaging in the various doggie activities that Brian the trainer provided.

Molly

While Tilly excelled at agility and search and rescue, the others were, shall we say, a little less proficient at the activities, though that didn't prevent them, or us from having some fun and laughs at their antics.

While Tilly excelled at virtually every activity at the training sessions, the exception being Flyball, (she was fast, but just wouldn't give the ball back once she had it in her mouth), the others weren't quite so clever. We thought Dylan would be great at agility, but though he was quite good at negotiating the various obstacles while on the lead and being led around the course, once he was set free, he took the opportunity to set off on a long, fast run, all round the training field, much to everyone's amusement. His Bedlington 'speed genes' certainly kicked in on those occasions, and it could take up to five minutes to retrieve and get him back on his lead.

Charlie and Molly quickly made it clear that they weren't at all interested in Flyball, agility, or any of the other activities Brian introduced for fun at the end of the sessions. They were great at all the obedience lessons, but anything else just wasn't their thing. Still, we all had fun at the Saturday afternoon training sessions and everyone was quite excited when, one day, Brian announced that, starting the following week, we'd be holding the sessions, once a month at the very large wood that stood close to the town's racecourse. This would give the dogs the opportunity to take part in various activities in a natural environment and would hopefully be even greater fun for all concerned.

When I told Juliet about the new arrangement, she was interested to see how Brian intended to conduct these sessions and she said she'd come with us the following week. We dutifully turned up for the training in the woods and a good crowd of other owners and their dogs were there too.

We did lots of simple exercises, obedience being a feature. It's much harder to get a dog to come back to you when you hide behind a tree and call him, and he or she has to search for you. In general, all the dogs did well and definitely seemed to be enjoying their afternoon in the woods.

Then, Brian announced he wanted us to do long-distance recall. When it was Tilly's turn, Carol, Brian's partner, led her to a point about 400 yards along the straight woodland path, to where a small bridge crossed one of the many dykes that run through the wood. When she gave me the prearranged signal, I shouted , "Tilly, come here," and little Tilly set off, at top speed, running straight as an arrow along the path, until she was a few yards from me, when I simply held a hand up, and she came to a halt, right in front of my feet. Everyone was so impressed; they gave Tilly a spontaneous round of applause. Her tail wagged as if she was taking a bow, and then it was the turn of Molly, who repeated the exercise at a sedate pace, taking over a minute to reach me, but at least she did it, as did Charlie, who gave virtually a carbon copy of Molly's performance.

At last it was Dylan's turn, and I turned to Brian and said, "Brian, I'm not sure this is a good idea. Dylan's sense of recall isn't the best in the world, and I'm worried in case he won't come back."

"Don't worry," Brian reassured me. "With you, Juliet and the girls here, and all his dog friends, there shouldn't be a problem."

Reluctantly, I allowed Carol to walk Dylan along the path to the bridge over the dyke. She and Dylan looked so small from that distance, and I feared the worst. I saw Dylan sitting perfectly by her side. She lifted her arm and then, when she saw my acknowledging wave, her arm dropped, the signal to begin.

"Dylan, come here," I literally bawled at the top of my voice, making sure he couldn't fail to hear me.

Carol released him and Dylan took off like an express train … in the opposite direction!

"Dylan," I called again, louder than ever, with no response from the little fella who had by now disappeared into the trees. Rebecca and Victoria were both almost hysterical, shouting his name and any other words their young minds could think of that might entice him to return to us. Juliet tried to calm them down. She told them Dylan was too far away to be able to hear their voices by that time. Somehow, that made things worse.

As Brian mustered everyone to go in search of Dylan, I couldn't resist making a short, barbed remark.

"I told you so."

"I honestly didn't think he'd do that," he replied, and I resisted the urge to say any more. My priority was to find our little boy and get him safely back on his lead. The big problem as far as I was concerned was that the wood, a local tourist attraction, covers a total of 140 acres, and includes miles and miles of footpaths, all running in different directions through the wood, a separate 3.6 mile hiking trail, various picnic areas, and numerous dykes, most containing stagnant, muddy water. With thousands of trees, there were literally almost endless places where Dylan could be, and of course there was no guarantee that a dog would stick to the paths.

The other dog owners were split into search parties and everybody began enthusiastically searching for the runaway. After about twenty minutes, someone reported having seen Dylan bounding through the trees, chasing a squirrel that had run up a tree. Some of us made our way to the area where he'd been seen, and thus began a search that would eventually last nearly 90 minutes with people, Juliet and I included, catching various quick sightings of the errant Dylan, who was apparently having a wonderful time, chasing squirrels to his heart's content, deliberately choosing to ignore all calls for him to return to us or anyone else. Maybe he was suffering from a case of selective deafness! My biggest fear was that he'd jump into one of the dykes and find himself immersed in the horrible black, smelly water. The thought of cleaning a dog covered in that stuff didn't bear thinking about.

After about an hour of the chase, a few of the other owners had to leave and go home. It was well past the time when the training session should have ended, and they understandably had other things to do. A few stayed to continue the search and we were very grateful for their help.

It had turned into what could have been a scene from a comedy film. People were traipsing through the woods, calling his name and looking for him, whilst every now and then, someone would catch sight of him as he crossed the trail they were on, sometimes only a few yards ahead, as he zoomed around in search of the elusive squirrels.

I'd seen him at least three times and been unable to attract his attention. He was obviously too focussed on enjoying himself. Finally, I turned to Brian and said,

"I've had an idea. If we don't try something new, we could still be chasing him around these woods in the dark."

"What's your idea?" he asked.

"What about seeing just how good Tilly is at search and rescue? Let's send her to find him, and hopefully, if she does, he'll follow her back to us."

"It's worth a try," he replied, "as long as we don't end up losing Tilly too."

"There's no chance of that, Tilly's too devoted to me to run away."

Brian agreed it was worth a go, and I simply turned to Tilly, and in hope and anticipation, said, "Tilly, go find Dylan."

I let her off her lead and she took off along the path, then after a hundred yards or so, she suddenly veered off to the left and disappeared into the trees. I kept my fingers crossed. We'd taken a big chance, because after all, it was a big wood, and the question was, had Tilly understood what I'd instructed her to do?

After about ten minutes, someone suddenly shouted... "Look there, on the bridge."

We'd arrived back at the place where we'd originally started the exercise, and sure enough, when we looked along the path to the bridge over the dyke where Carol had released the dogs, we saw Tilly sitting on the bridge, waiting for me, with Dylan by her side. She'd done it! Tilly had succeeded where all of us humans had failed in almost two hours of searching.

I didn't want to take a chance on Dylan doing a runner for a second time, so I simply shouted, "Stay," and slowly walked where the two dogs sat, and, having reached them without

Dylan taking off again, I clipped his lead on and led him back along the path, with Tilly walking off-lead by my side, looking very pleased with herself. Rebecca and Victoria were holding onto Molly and Charlie's leads. Those two had been extremely good dogs, probably loving the extra-long walk they'd been treated to that day. Juliet had a look of pure relief on her face as we arrived back at our original point of origin and took Dylan's lead from me as I clipped Tilly back onto hers.

What else could we do but tell Dylan what a good boy he was, for coming (eventually) back. Telling him off would only have lessened the chances of him ever coming back when recalled in future. It was one of things Brian taught in his obedience classes. Put yourself in your dog's mind. Would you happily go running back to someone if you thought you were going to get shouted at or hit when you got there? Especially in Dylan's case with his history of abuse, that would be extremely counter-productive.

Anyway, it wasn't really Dylan's fault, was it, as I now pointed out again to Brian, the trainer.

"I don't like to say I told you so," I said to him. "But we could have saved ourselves a lot of time and trouble if you'd listened to me and not insisted we let him off his lead."

"I know, I know," he replied, looking a little sheepish. That's appropriate, don't you think, sheepish/Bedlington terrier…get it?

"In future, unless we're in the confines of the training field, Dylan stays on the lead, agreed?"

"Agreed," he responded, immediately. He turned to the remaining dog owners who'd stayed to help in searching for Dylan and thanked them for staying to aid in the search, and I thanked them too. All of them replied that it was the least they could do. After all, they were dog lovers too, and couldn't bear to think of anything bad happening to someone else's dog.

As they all filtered off to return to their cars with their dogs, Juliet and the girls, and I turned around and were just about to leave when Brian spoke to us again.

"Will we still see you next week at regular training?"

"Of course you will. What made you think otherwise?" I replied. He obviously thought we might abandon his training classes because of the Dylan incident as it became known.

"Oh, nothing," he said. "Just thought that after today..."

"Don't be daft, Brian," I interrupted him. "We're not so stupid as to hold one little incident against you. Anyway, look at Dylan's face, he hasn't had such a good time as this since the day he was born, I'll wager."

Everyone looked at Dylan. It was true. If ever a dog could be said to look happy it was him. Somehow, he managed to look as if he'd just had the time of his life. He wasn't even panting or breathless from almost two hours of chasing squirrels and generally exploring all around the woods. God knows how many miles our little boy had covered during his afternoon on the run, but it certainly didn't seem to have done him any harm. We stayed to discuss other training related matters with Brian and Carol for a few minutes before we loaded our dogs into the back of the Mondeo and left for home.

The afternoon in the woods had certainly been an experience, one we wouldn't forget for a long, long time, or, as it's being mentioned here, for ever!

Tilly and Dylan - Hero and Villain

There was one thing that Dylan's little escapade led to, and that was the new nickname he earned for himself. From that day, and even now, within the family he is known as 'Dylan the Villain'.

6

DYLAN AT THE NATIONAL SHOW

WHEN WE ADOPTED DYLAN, despite him being under-sized and under-nourished, we were very proud of our little Bedlington Terrier, or Beddie, as they are affectionately known. So much so that I enrolled in the National Bedlington Terrier Club UK. Of course, we had no intention of showing him, in dog shows obviously. He wasn't that kind of dog. We didn't have his pedigree papers and in his condition he was as far from a show dog as you could possibly imagine.

One of the benefits of belonging to the society was that we received their regular magazine, which told of all things Bedlington related. In the first issue we received I saw that the magazine invited members to send in their Bedlington terrier related stories. I thought it would be nice to send them Dylan's story, as I didn't think too many Beddies suffered from the neglect and abuse Dylan had experienced. They are, after all a prestige breed, Bedlington puppies are very expensive, and it was hard to imagine anyone paying so much a pedigree puppy and then subjecting it to such appalling treatment.

So, I went ahead and wrote a three-page article about Dylan and sent it to them, not really expecting to hear from them. Much to my surprise and delight, a couple of weeks later I received a response from the secretary of the club. She was grateful to me for sending Dylan's story and she stressed to me that the club is for ALL Bedlington terrier owners, not just the ones with show dogs and told me they would be publishing Dylan's story in the next issue of the magazine. She asked me to send a photograph of Dylan that they could include in the article.

She then went on to tell me about the National Bedlington Terrier Club's annual show, which would be taking place quite soon. It was being held in Selby in Yorkshire, not too far from our home, and she invited us to take Dylan along, and enclosed the necessary forms to admit him to the show. The forms explained that all dogs entering the show area had to be officially registered and that Dylan fell into the category 'Not for Show'.

Juliet and I talked it over and decided it might be nice to go along and see all the 'posh' dogs on display at the show. Neither of us had ever attended an official organised dog show although

Juliet had taken part in many horse shows in her younger days, when she owned and rode her own horses. I duly filled in the forms, sent them off and a couple of weeks later, we received the list of entries for the show. There, along with all the long pedigree names with their previous awards and trophies listed under their names, was just one entry 'Not for Show'; our Dylan. I felt quite proud to see his name, just the one word, among what must have been all the most illustrious names in the Bedlington Terrier world of show dogs.

The day before the show, Dylan had to suffer being bathed and showered, dried and brushed and groomed within a hair of his life, as Juliet wanted him to look his best when he met all those 'posh dogs' the next day. I must admit, she did a damn fine job. Dylan looked great and we spent the rest of the day trying to prevent him getting dirty or messing up his neatly groomed coat, but Dylan's a dog, and dogs will be dogs. By the next morning, he required another spot of pampering, as Juliet again went to work to get him looking his best.

"He's not actually in the show. You don't need to go to all that trouble," I pointed out to her, and in response, was met with a withering look from my darling wife who went on to tell me,

"He might not be in the show, but he's going to be at the show. and from the look of that list of entries we received, our Dylan is going to be the only 'Not for Show' dog there. I don't want anyone looking down their noses at him, or laughing at him, just because he doesn't look like their snooty show winners and so on."

I felt immensely proud of Juliet at that moment. She was obviously determined that Dylan would look his very best and not be an object of fun or derision from anybody. She had experience in the show world with her horses and she assured me that people in those circles can often be quite bitchy and catty.

Not only Dylan, the girls had to look at their best, so Juliet next set about ensuring their hair was perfect, (they both had very long hair), and made sure they were nicely dressed for the occasion.

I asked her if she wanted to check me over too and received a playful slap on the back of my head for my trouble.

The time came for us to set off on our journey to Selby. We said our goodbyes to the rest of our dogs, who would oversee the house for a few hours, and with Dylan looking out of the rear window, we were soon on our way. It was show time!

We were blessed with fine weather for our day out. The sun was shining with barely a cloud in a beautiful blue sky, perfect for a drive through the country. Tilly and the others could be safely left in charge of the house for four hours or so, the maximum time we'd leave them unsupervised. With Selby no more than half an hour away by car, that meant an hour's travelling time there and back, leaving us up to three hours at the show, plenty of time to see what we wanted to.

Arriving in Selby, we passed the beautiful Minster church, Selby Abbey, which dates back to the 11th century, and which dominates the Selby skyline. Following the map provided by the club, we soon found the venue for the show and easily found a space in the car park. Alighting from the car, we extricated Dylan from the back; he'd been a perfect dog on the journey, happily watching the passing scenery from the rear windows and once out of the car, we walked him round the edges of the car park, in case he needed the toilet.

That done, we walked towards the entrance of the hall where the show was being held and as we were about to enter through the main door, we were held up by a man who I can only describe as resembling a real-life Lord Snooty, the famous character who featured in the Beano comic. As we soon found out, he not only looked like Lord Snooty, he also behaved like him.

With an air of superiority, he attempted to prevent us entering the building.

"You can't come in here," he said with a supercilious grin on his face, obviously enjoying his power to allow or deny entry to his precious show. "Only official entries are allowed within the hall."

I'd met people like him many times during my lifetime, and I wasn't going to allow him to intimidate me or my family, or more importantly, Dylan!

"Is that right?" I asked, safe in the knowledge I had the beating of this self-important little man, who stood at no more than five foot six.

"Yes, it is," he replied curtly, looking down his nose at Dylan as he spoke.

"That's alright then," I said firmly and confidently. "Dylan *is* an official entry."

He almost sputtered as he seemed to choke on his words. He should have seen that Juliet and I both wore club badges, identifying us as members. If he'd seen them, he should at least have been a little more respectful.

"He is? But how...?

"He's a Not for Show entry. I suggest you check your list of entries, or would you like to see mine?" I held up my official entry list, virtually waving it in his face. "Look at the last page." I ordered the bumptious official.

Before he could consult his copy of the list of entries, however, a lady came almost bouncing out through the door and immediately exclaimed.

"Oh, this must be Dylan and you're Mr and Mrs Porter, right?

It turned out that this lady was the club secretary, the one who'd corresponded with me and who'd invited us to bring Dylan along to the show.

She went down, virtually on her knees and made a great fuss of Dylan. Then straightening up, she said to me,

"I'm so pleased you've brought him to see us today. As I said in my letter, the club is for all Bedlington owners, not just those who show their dogs. Turning to 'Lord Snooty' she said, "You must have seen the article about Dylan being rescued from a life of abuse by Mr and Mrs Porter in the recent club magazine?"

He obviously hadn't but blustered a little, then replied, "Oh yes, of course. So sorry."

His last words were directed at Juliet and I, and I was gracious enough to accept his apology. Just then another couple arrived, with their very posh-looking dog in tow.

"Howay, man, this must be Dylan," the man said, in a distinctive Geordie accent. He and his wife had driven down from Newcastle for the show. "We read about him in the club mag. Great to meet you," and he shook hands with Juliet and me.

His wife was making a big fuss of Dylan, while their dog sat peacefully at her side.

The man introduced himself and his wife and their dog. I don't remember its pedigree or show name, but its everyday name was Patsy.

"Come with us, man," he told us, and we'll show you around. With that, and with the club secretary following, we marched into the hall, with Dylan beside us, leaving 'Lord Snooty' resembling a fish, mouth gawping, as we swept past him.

Our new acquaintances spent a few minutes showing us around and introduced us to a few of the people they knew, then left us to explore the show hall by ourselves. There were a few stalls, selling dog related products; food, collars and leads, dog coats etc. but what interested us most of all were the tables set up all round the hall, each of which held a Bedlington terrier being groomed or generally smartened up ready for showing by its owner.

We stopped to talk with a few, but some were too busy to engage in conversation. Those we quickly bypassed. Without exception, the ones we did manage to speak with had never met a rescued Beddie before and were interested in hearing about Dylan. Some had read my article in the club magazine, and some were hearing about Dylan for the first time. Juliet and I were pleased that people showed an interest in Dylan. They could easily have been too 'stuck-up' to bother with a little, undersized, scruffy version of their perfectly presented show dogs.

Poor Victoria, however, received a bit of a shock at one table, when after stopping to admire the dog, standing in a perfect show pose, she innocently reached out to try and stoke the dog's head.

"Stop!" the dog's lady owner almost shouted her order to Victoria, who was only about 7 or 8 at the time. Victoria just about jumped out of her skin. When she stepped back the lady said, "Sorry if I scared you, but it's taken me over an hour to get his head looking like that. I can't risk him being messed up before the show."

Juliet apologised for Victoria who seemed on the verge of tears. She soon cheered up as we progressed round the hall and met some really nice people, none more so than one man who was putting the finishing touches to grooming his extremely handsome male Beddie, who looked as if he'd just jumped off the pages of a glossy fashion magazine, which we soon learned...he had!

* * *

THE DOG'S owner was a really nice man, who was only too pleased to talk to us. He listened with great interest as Juliet related Dylan's story to him and expressed his admiration of us for adopting him after all he'd gone through in his early life. Juliet and I were really interested in learning about his amazingly gorgeous dog. He explained that his dog, whose name I sadly don't remember had recently been awarded Best in Breed at Crufts and was the previous year's 'Best in Show' at the equivalent of that day's show.

He then reached under the table and brought out a box containing several glossy magazines. Opening a couple to certain marked pages, he showed us his dog in different adverts for expensive and exclusive products and explained that he was under contract to various companies for his services in advertising their products. Truly, a lucrative side-line for him and his dog.

Juliet then asked him a question, one to which the answer would change Dylan's life, well, his hairstyle at least. She asked him how to make Dylan look a bit more like the dogs at the show, in other words, how to get the distinctive sheep appearance around his head.

This very nice man told her to put Dylan up on his table, next to his dog, which she did. He then picked up a pair of scissors and a brush and commenced giving her a half-hour masterclass in Bedlington grooming and clipping. He explained each step along the way, and before we knew it, he'd transformed Dylan's appearance completely. Gone was our scruffy looking pseudo-Bedlington, having been replaced by a typical, every day, normal and instantly recognisable Beddie. I hadn't realised that a few people had stopped to watch as well and as our new friend stepped back, those people broke into a polite round of applause.

Dylan looked great! Juliet and I were stunned at the change, brought about in such a short space of time. We thanked the man effusively, but he just shrugged it off and said he was happy to help. He then went over a couple of things with Juliet once again to make sure she'd grasped the subtleties of what he'd showed her, and then picked Dylan up and placed him on the floor once more, where our little boy had a good shake and stood wagging his tail, as if he knew he now looked like every other dog in the hall.

Cameras weren't permitted in the venue so we were unable to take a picture of him immediately following his transformation and had to wait until we got home to take a photo, and also show him off to our friends and doggie acquaintances, when either of us took him out for his walks.

Dylan - Mark 2

We said thank you (again) to our friendly man with the Crufts winning dog and carried on going around the various exhibits on display at the show. All too soon, our time at the show was almost up, but we had enough time left to watch the judging of the first classification of the day. It was so interesting to watch all those gorgeous dogs being paraded and pit through their paces in the show ring, and we joined in the applause for the winners.

Then, it really was time to leave. We had to think of our other dogs at home, so reluctantly, we sought out the club secretary and thanked her for inviting us, the Geordie couple with Patsy, and a few of the other people we'd talked to during the day, who all thanked us for attending and letting them meet Dylan, which was really nice of them.

We even got a smile from 'Lord Snooty' as we walked from the hall into the car park. He was still diligently 'standing guard' at the main entrance, ensuring no unauthorised dogs gained entrance to the show area.

In what felt like no time at all, we arrived home and received the usual ecstatic greetings from Tilly, Charlie and Molly. I'm not sure, but I could almost swear that Tilly gave Dylan a long, hard stare as she took in his new appearance. Did she approve? We'll never know unfortunately.

It was back to normal from the time we arrived home. All the dogs needed walking and of course, Juliet insisted on taking Dylan to show him off to her 'doggie' friends, who she usually met up with on the large playing field near our home in the afternoon. We used to call it the 'dog club' and it's still going on to this day. When she returned from her walk, she told me that her friends were so impressed with Dylan's new look. A couple of them even thought we'd got a new dog!

Later that evening, after all the excitement of the day, she turned to me and said,

"You know, there's only one drawback about today."

"What's that," I asked, feeling very curious.

"Now that kind man has shown me how to make Dylan look like a real Bedlington, I'm going to have to work hard to keep him looking like that."

"I know there's lot of work involved in achieving the look," I replied, "but I'm sure you'll manage it."

And she has. Dylan always looks good, and she has spent many hours over the years keeping him like that. Juliet even went on to do a dog grooming course, which she passed, to enable her to keep all our dogs looking their best.

For now though, Dylan had had his day at the National Show and as far as we were concerned it had been a great success, and we would remember the man who'd taught Juliet the skill of clipping Dylan into shape for a very long time, with immense gratitude for his unselfish act of kindness.

7

FLYING TONIGHT!

AS TIME PASSED and Dylan grew to maturity it became obvious that he'd inherited the Bedlington speed gene. When we went on the small playing field near our home, not the larger one that Juliet visited in the afternoon, I was able to let him off his lead to stretch his legs. If she was off school, Victoria would often accompany me on these walks, and we'd have great fun watching Dylan enjoying the freedom to run free. It was during one of these walks that I took a photo that defined Dylan for us in so many ways, When we got home after our walk and looked at the photo I'd taken of him running across the field, Victoria suddenly pointed something out to me,

"Look, Brian. Dylan's flying!"

I took a close look at the photo to try and see what she meant by her remark. Sure enough, when looked at closely, you can see that I somehow managed to capture Dylan in the millisecond or so when all four of his paws were clear of the ground.

"You're right," Laughed as I replied to Victoria's astute observation. "It's Dylan the Flying Bedlington."

Dylan looked so happy as he ran at top speed across that playing field and I think you can see the sheer happiness of the moment beautifully captured in the photo, tail up, tongue out and his ears flapping.

The flying Bedlington!

Dylan was loving life, and we were all delighted to have witnessed the transformation from that nervous, timid dog, to a confident, happy and assertive boy who had even begun to bark at any dog that upset him. The only problem was, and is, Dylan's bark. It really is an annoying sound to hear his high-pitched bark, which happens to be loud enough to wake the dead. Once he starts, it's often difficult to get him to stop. It's as if one day, he found his bark, and now likes to hear the sound of his own voice!

Although he was still a young dog, Dylan also had one particular health issue that had dogged him, (excuse the pun) from the time we first adopted him. Despite only being 11 months old when he came to us, Dylan had always had bad teeth, which our vet put down to the abuse and poor diet he was undoubtedly fed as a puppy. In fact, when compared with other Beddies of a similar age, he looked small and under-nourished, and even today, at almost 15 years of age, he's still light as a feather, and can easily be picked up with one hand.

Back to his teeth, however, and it was his vet who mentioned this to me when I took Dylan along for his annual booster when he was five years old. He explained that Dylan had significant plaque build-up on his teeth and suggested daily brushing to help the problem. I bought a good quality dog toothbrush and paste and every day, I would brush his teeth to the best of my ability, which wasn't an easy task as Dylan hated having his teeth brushed. He made it very difficult for me to hold his mouth open with one hand whilst brushing with the other. The job might have been easier if I'd possessed a third arm. After a couple of months of unsuccessfully trying to improve his dental hygiene, I admitted defeat and booked him in to see the vet again and asked him if there were any alternatives to brushing that might have a more positive effect.

He told me that they could take Dylan in for a day, and under anaesthetic, his teeth could be scaled and polished, just like we humans have done at the dentist. The only thing most people baulked at was the cost of the procedure. As dental work wasn't covered by Dylan's pet insurance, we would be responsible for the full cost of the procedure which would be approximately £150. (Around $200 dollars at the time). I phoned Juliet from the veterinary surgery for her input and she agreed that it would be good idea to have it done, as it might also prolong the life of his teeth, so I agreed and we booked Dylan in for the procedure in a week's time.

On the day of the procedure, I dropped Dylan off at the surgery first thing in the morning and arranged to collect him later that day. It wasn't as if he was having an invasive operation or surgical procedure, but he would be having a general anaesthetic, so we couldn't help worrying a little about our little Beddie, and it was a great relief when I received a phone call around lunch time, informing me that Dylan was all done and awake after the anaesthetic, and that I could pick him up any time I wanted.

An hour later I drove the four miles to the surgery and checked in to collect our boy. Soon after I was called into a consulting room and Dylan was brought through to me. He was extremely excited to see me and began leaping around the room, like a spring lamb, something he always does when he's really happy. He virtually leaped up into my arms, such was his joy at seeing me again. When he finally calmed down, we were able to lift him onto the examination table so that I could have a look at his teeth. They'd certainly done a good job. Dylan's teeth were sparkling by comparison to the way they had appeared a few hours previously and Juliet agreed once Dylan and I returned home a short time later.

In an effort to maintain his new-look teeth, we decided to give him a daily denta-stick. They are sold after all, as means of helping to clean your dog's teeth and helping reduce plaque and gun disease. Anything was worth a try after spending all that money just to clean his teeth. Dylan really loved his denta-sticks, which I gave him every day, after tea in an evening. Whether they've actually helped his teeth it's hard to say, because he's still having one a day after all these years, and despite us paying to have his teeth cleaned again a few years ago, the plaque soon returns again. I'm pretty certain his gums and teeth were irrevocably damaged when he was a puppy, poorly fed, beaten, and just not receiving the necessary vitamins and protein to build a healthy body and teeth.

Most Beddies I've met over the years tend to be almost twice Dylan's size and from speaking to their owners, fully grown dogs weigh anything from 9 up to about 12 kilograms.

Dylan weighs on average between 8 and 9 kilos, and is very skinny, but fit as a fiddle.

Meanwhile, life went on as normal for Dylan, who continued to astound everyone who met him with his speed when let off his lead. It was quite funny to see how he reacted as I unclipped his lead. Instead of standing still or walking around for a minute, he'd instantly jump up as high as he could, as if he was on springs, twist round and round in circles as if he was winding himself up, like a spring, and then he'd suddenly break into a run, zooming away and then covering the whole area of the playing field in ever decreasing circles, occasionally stopping to get his bearings, and then dashing off again, all accompanied by great vocal encouragement from Victoria and me, and anyone else who happened to be with us, sharing our time on the field.

Sometimes he'd take his ball for a run, too! He loved playing with a ball from time to time but was at his happiest playing with a soft toy. More of that later!

Go Dylan, go!

8

CHANGING FACES

AS I MENTIONED in the introduction to this story, Dylan has been with us longer than any of our dogs. Because of that one fact, he has seen several comings and goings among the members of our rescue family. As time passed, we'd had to say tearful goodbyes to Tilly, Charlie, Molly and some that haven't been mentioned in this story. I'm not going into details about those who've left us, as I don't want Dylan's story to become a repetitive tale of loss and sadness.

I'll just say that each and every dog who has been a part of our family, some longer than others, has been a much loved, and now, sadly missed member of our rescue pack, and their presence in our home has helped to enrich our lives and our hearts, with their love, their faithfulness and their at times, hilarious antics. Rescue dogs are definitely a special breed. They seem to know when they've been given a second, often third chance of a happy life and they repay the faith you the love you give to them, a hundred times over.

So it was that our pack underwent significant changes in the last few years, with some new faces joining us that are recognisable to those who follow my Facebook pages as our current pack.

One name that has been with us almost as long as Dylan, is little Cassie, aka The Mad Ferret, our manic Yorkie/Australian terrier cross breed. Her story is told in *Cassie's Tale*, book 3 in this series. Cassie is kind of like a Duracell bunny, but without an 'off' switch. This little pocket dynamo of a dog, despite being fifteen years old, never stops running, is full of energy, and bosses all the other dogs around, is an expert ball thief, does a funny kind of 'hand stand' on her front paws when she does a wee, and has an attitude far bigger than her actual body size. This is despite having had two operations in recent years for ruptured cruciate ligaments, in each of her back legs, and even that hasn't slowed her down.

Cassie was very closely followed into our home by Penny, the Jack Russell crossbreed, whose story I've also related in book 4 in the series, *Penny the Railway Pup*. This little girl is also approaching fifteen this year and after being abandoned and left cruelly tied to a railway line, she eventually found her forever home with us, and has led an eventful life, to put it mildly.

So, Dylan had some new friends and perhaps because they were of a similar age, he got on right away with Cassie and Penny, who have become his firm friends over the years. Juliet and I often joke that they are our OAPD trio, (*That's Old Age Pensioner Dog*).

Only a few months went by before the family expanded once again, with the adoption of former bait dog, Sheba, who'd been horrendously abused and finally thrown on a rubbish tip and left to die. Not much more than a living skeleton when she joined us, Sheba wasn't expected to live more than a few months, but with love and expert care, she's now thirteen years old, and despite suffering from arthritis, is still going strong, and is a much loved and loving family pet, and she's the fourth member of our 'old codgers' brigade.

Sheba's story is told in the second book in the Family of Rescuedogs series, *Sheba: From Hell to Happiness,* and her at times harrowing, no punches pulled tale is a repeat bestseller in the UK, USA and Australia, with many 5 star reviews from readers, many moved to tears by her story.

The 'Old Codgers' – Sheba, Penny, Cassie & Dylan

The whole dynamic of our little rescue family was gradually changing with the passage of time, and Dylan was proving his adaptability by his acceptance into 'his' home of these new additions to the family.

The addition of Sheba to our family highlighted to Juliet and me, the plight of the many Staffordshire Bull Terriers in rescue centres all over the country, and we decided to do something about it, in our own small way. Subsequently we added Dexter, the beautiful black Labrador/Staffy crossbreed, who'd been thrown from a moving car on a motorway, and who recently passed away at the age of twelve. His story was recently told in book 5 of the series, *Remembering Dexter*, possibly the most emotional book I've ever written, and which was written by public demand, after his death, as so many people had followed his last, year long illness and when he died, a large number of his fans asked me to write his life story.

Juliet wanted to adopt a staffy puppy, and we visited our local sanctuary, where we'd found Dylan, and as if fate had decreed it, they had two staffy puppies needing homes. They'd been part of an abandoned litter, and like Dylan, they'd been abandoned at the gates of the sanctuary. Most of the litter had been rehomed, but one boy and one girl remained.

We decided to take the little boy dog, by then he and his sister were six months old, and because of the snuffling noise he made when we made a fuss of him, we named him Muttley, after the *Whacky Races* cartoon dog. Perhaps because he'd spent the first six months of his life in the sanctuary, and never having experienced living in a house before, he was a difficult dog to house train. Teaching him to ask to go outside for the toilet took far longer than was usual for a puppy, but the biggest problem we faced with Muttley was...chewing!

Muttley chewed anything, whatever he could get sink his teeth into...he chewed. I think, in his first six months with us, he chewed and destroyed six beds, countless dog toys and worst of all he started on the house itself. He chewed all the skirting boards in the kitchen, the bottoms of doors, and just about every blanket we added to his bed. In the garden, he destroyed numerous plants and tried chewing his way through quite several plant pots. He was like a one-dog demolition team.

Gradually, applying a great deal of patience and with repetitive training, we began to cure this worst trait in his character.

Dexter and Muttley

Dylan took it all in his stride. When a new dog arrived in our home, Dylan would carry on as if nothing had happened, neither greeting nor rejecting the new dog. It was as if he just wasn't bothered how many dogs he had to live with as long as they left him alone to do his own thing.

One thing that pleased us immensely, as the years passed, was that Dylan appeared to have cast off the fears and nervousness that had affected his early days with us. In fact, he now relished human contact. He loved nothing better than jumping up on my knee, or Juliet's as we sat in the lounge in an evening, and virtually draping himself around our shoulders, where he'd happily go to sleep, and whoever he was with would be reluctant to move and wake him up. We nicknamed him, Dylan the Scarf when he did this, because that's exactly what he looked like, a nice, warm and furry scarf.

At other times he'd just love to curl up on my lap, (or Juliet's), almost cat-like and he'd lie there until disturbed. While he was lying like that, I'd just sit watching TV or reading perhaps whilst gently stroking him with my free hand. He'd curl up even tighter and the sound of his gentle breathing as he lay there was quite therapeutic. The amazing thing about Dylan is that he could curl up into the smallest of spaces. He'd sometimes jump onto the chair where I sat, and if another of the dogs was already on my knee, he'd slide between my legs and the side of the armchair and before I knew it he'd be curled up in a tight ball in the tiny space, happily dozing beside me.

Of course, at the end of the day, he loved nothing more than snuggling down, and falling asleep in his nice, warm comfy bed.

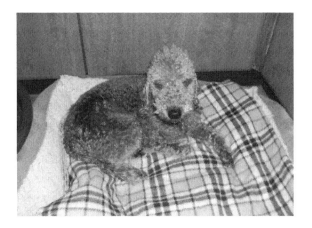

Nite nite

9

SEA DOG

I'M sure many of my readers will have already read *Penny the Railway Pup*, book 4 in this series. If you have, the following chapter will sound extremely familiar to you. That's because our day at the seaside with Dylan and Penny was covered in Penny's story, but as it's as much Dylan's story as it is Penny's, it's only fair to include it here. Of course, if you haven't read Penny's book this will be all new to you. Either way, I hope you enjoy the tale of our visit to the seaside, of fish and chips, seagulls and sea monsters!

One nice autumn day, we decided to visit Juliet's two eldest children (both adults by now), who lived and worked in Scarborough, on the east coast, a hugely popular holiday resort. With it being a warm, sunny day, we decided to take a couple of the dogs with us, and we decided to take Dylan and Penny with us. They were both small and good travellers in the car, (we thought), so were ideal for a day at the seaside. Our friend, Ken offered to dog sit for us, so we wouldn't have to dash back too soon.

The journey was a nightmare. Juliet and I were in the front

of the car, Rebecca and Victoria in the back and the two dogs in the rear of the estate car. We stopped at a rest point about halfway through our journey of round about 80 miles, to let the dogs out for a walkabout, and to go to the toilet. Opening the tailgate, we discovered that one of the dogs had been sick. Was it Penny or Dylan? As Dylan had travelled many times in the car, we guessed that Penny had to be the culprit. The second half of the journey saw me pulling over at least five times, as Penny continued vomiting every few minutes, and each time we let her out of the car, she ran to the grass verge beside the road to try and eat grass, and if she peed once, she must have done so at least a dozen during that awful last few miles.

We finally arrived at our destination and our first stop was at the farm owned and operated as a livery yard by Juliet's friend, Sheila, her best friend from the time she lived in the resort herself.

The dogs loved walking around on the farm, all the new sights and smells must have been heavenly to their doggie senses. Dylan in particular loved walking along the lane that led from the livery stable to the road, seeing the horses in the fields, and I loved the commanding views that the walk afforded me from the farm's setting high above the town itself. He and I enjoyed a lovely, peaceful walk, taking in all the sights, sounds and smells of the countryside. Even though Scarborough is a fairly large seaside resort town, it is surrounded by the beautiful countryside of the North Yorkshire Moors, a National Park with many beautiful villages and areas of open country and forestry to explore, and the countryside begins within a couple of miles of the outskirts of the town.

Penny, however, barked almost non-stop and tried her best to chase the horses, much to our surprise. Penny had been brought up in close proximity to Lisa's two horses, without causing a problem, and there were quite often horses on the rough scrubland that bordered the large playing field at home, and Penny had never once made any attempt to chase or disturb them. Maybe the sea air was playing havoc with her senses. Was it the strange smells of the farm, or the fact she'd suffered from an upset tummy on the journey that were causing her unusual behaviour? Whatever the reason, we felt compelled to put her back on her lead and she spent the rest of our time at the farm under close supervision. Penny was in disgrace!

After staying long enough to sit and have a coffee and a good long chat with Sheila, we left the farm and made our way into town to visit Juliet's son, Robert and daughter, Rachel. They'd both managed to take some time off work to spend with us, and it was so nice for Juliet to get to share some time with them.

Both dogs were loving their day out, and the sea air was doing us all a power of good. Penny was her usual self again once we left the farm, and there was no repeat of her earlier sickness as we drove the short distance into the town and headed for the sea front, luckily finding a parking space within a few yards of the beach. During the summer, dogs are banned from the beach at Scarborough, but, luckily for us, the official tourist season had just ended, and we were able to take them both for a great walk and to play on the sands. It was obviously the first time either dog had felt the sensation of sand under their paws, as both were a little tentative at first, as they felt the warm softness of the beach beneath their feet, but soon got used to it and began to enjoy themselves.

Great fun!

We started our walk at one end of the beach, which began beside what was the outer wall of one side of the harbour wall. Scarborough's harbour is a busy port, being home to a small fleet of trawlers, as well as several popular pleasure 'steamers' which provided tourists and holidaymakers with trips along the coast. Still referred to as steamers, these vessels are nowadays powered by modern diesel engines and no longer send plumes of smoke into the air from their funnels as they sail along.

For those who don't know Scarborough well, or at all, I should mention that it is one of England's most popular holiday resorts. Situated on the east coast, it has two bays, both with sandy beaches, which are split by a headland, on top of which stand the ruins of the 12th century Scarborough Castle, commissioned by King Henry II, and an important Royal fortification in guarding England's east coast against invaders from Scandinavia. The stone castle built by Henry replaced an earlier wooden fortification built by William le Gros, a powerful Anglo-Norman baron, a grand nephew of William the Conqueror. The castle was even shelled by a German Naval bombardment on 16th December 1914 when two German battleships, the *Derfflinger* and *Von der Tann*, fired more than 55 shells into the town and castle from Scarborough Bay, also striking the lighthouse and causing so much damage the tower had to be pulled down and was eventually rebuilt. Eighteen of the town's civilian population were killed during the bombardment.

Apart from the castle, the town also boasts a Sea Life Centre, which houses Yorkshire's only seal hospital and the world-renowned Peasholm Park, an oriental themed municipal park which even includes its own naval battle as one of its attractions, fought by remote controlled model warships, and a new, ultra-modern holiday complex, *The Sands,* managed by Juliet's eldest daughter, Rachel, and son Robert, situated right on the sea front, with stunning views over the sea. Since she's grown up, my youngest step-daughter, Victoria, has joined them, and now lives and works in Scarborough too, where she's learning the hospitality trade under the auspices of Rachel and Robert and where she also helps to take care of their dogs in her off-duty hours. She loves to come home regularly in her shiny new car, mostly to see the dogs, rather than her Mum and me. Sheba has always been special to Victoria, and when she was growing up, our little rescued Staffy used to sleep in Victoria's bedroom. Sheba had her own bed in the room, but very often, if Juliet or I peeped into the room before we turned in for the night, we'd see Sheba and Victoria, beautifully snuggled up in Victoria's bed, Victoria's arm usually draped across Sheba, keeping her safe and secure. Only later, when Victoria was in her teens, did Sheba begin to sleep downstairs again, as Victoria would often be out with her friends at night, and the dog's bedtime would come before she arrived home, so it was no longer practical for Sheba to share her room, especially if she had a friend sleeping over in her room. Whenever she comes home for a visit, Victoria always makes a big fuss of Sheba, and the other dogs of course, but there's no denying that there is a special bond between the two of them.

Scarborough is also home to one of the country's oldest

operational lifeboat stations, standing on the north pier, which is a popular visitor attraction in its own right. And now, let's return to our walk on the beach.

As I mentioned earlier, we began our walk beside the harbour wall, which also served as a wide promenade where people could sit and watch the world go by, see the ships entering or leaving the harbour, or perhaps sit on one of the benches provided, or on the wall itself, and eat their fish and chips, bought from one of many nearby Fish and Chip shops, serving freshly cooked, locally caught fish, mostly tasty cod or haddock. The presence of those enjoying their fish meals, and the newly docked trawlers also served to attract many seagulls that wheeled, screeched and swooped and often landed close enough for people to throw them a few scraps from their meal. Others landed on the beach, and began pecking at the sand, presumably seeking some tasty morsel or two, shellfish perhaps, buried in the sand, waiting for the coming of the next high tide.

On the beach

Dylan and Penny were now attracted by the screeching

and squawking of the gulls as they dived and swooped over-head. Penny decided to do her best to ignore them, or perhaps to imitate them, as she began to sniff at the sand and then started to use her front paws to start digging a nice hole in the beach.

We laughed, wondering what on earth she was trying to achieve. Whatever it was, she was enjoying herself, and that was all that mattered. Dylan, on the other hand, had higher thoughts in mind. By that comment, I really do mean *higher*. His attention was firmly fixed on the seagulls. This being his first visit to the coast, he'd obviously never seen or heard seag-ulls before. These very large flying monsters were nothing like the little sparrows and starlings that regularly visited the bird tables in our garden, where we daily place food for our local bird population. Oh no, these grey and white things that now flew and sometimes hovered above us must have seemed like beasts from another world to our little Bedlington terrier. The one thing I have to say about Dylan is that he is incredibly brave, can run like a greyhound and can leap like a gazelle.

Before we knew what was happening, he must have made his doggie mind up, and decided these large flying monsters were a threat that needed dealing with. Much to our amuse-ment he began leaping into the air, trying to catch the squadron of gulls that zoomed around above our heads. As one flew away, he'd turn his attention to another one and he would run and chase the next one in their formation, doing his best to catch one. As they had the advantage of flight, and were mostly at least twenty or thirty feet above him, he had no chance, but we couldn't really tell Dylan that, could we? He was having great fun trying! Juliet then caught my attention and told me to look up at the harbour wall.

A small crowd of holidaymakers, (and maybe some locals) had gathered to watch Dylan in his comical attempt to catch himself a seagull. The laughter was now easily heard from our position on the beach and of course, we could share in their amusement as they looked and pointed and even beckoned others to come and watch the little dog in his futile battle with the gulls. Rebeca and Victoria though it was hilarious, and everyone was clearly enjoying 'The Dylan Show' as he carried on for at least five minutes until a mixture of tiredness and boredom at his failure to catch a seagull probably signalled the end of his brave quest. That, plus the fact that most of the gulls had flown away, obviously seeking richer pickings further along the beach. When Dylan finally gave up his efforts, we were astounded when the sound of laughing from the harbour wall turned into a round of applause from some of those who'd enjoyed watching him. People shouted things like, "Better luck next time, fella," and "You need longer legs," and "Good try, young' un." We acknowledged the laughter and comments by waving to everyone, receiving many waves and blown kisses, (hopefully for Dylan), in return.

A paddle in the North Sea

As we turned to continue our walk along the beach we waved once more to the happy throng on the wall. Some of them, especially those who may have been on a day trip to the seaside, as we were, would probably remembered the crazy little dog that looked like a sheep cavorting around, chasing seagulls, for some time after they returned home that night.

It was only as we began walking away and proceeded further along the beach that I realised my cheeks were aching. I'd laughed so much myself, and Dylan had certainly enjoyed himself. Penny on the other hand, looked at us all as if we'd all gone mad. She'd succeeded in digging a couple of nice deep holes in the sand and had certainly enjoyed herself as much as Dylan had. Due to the possibility of him running off and trying to continue his seagull hunt, we kept Dylan on is lead as we progressed along the beach, but Penny was running free and seemed to have completely recovered from her upsetting car journey. We weren't really mad at her for her behaviour on the farm, as she was clearly excited and overwhelmed by the sight of so many horses in one place. We also knew she was just being playful and would never have tried to hurt the horses. Such a thing simply wasn't in her nature.

Now, however, it was her turn for some fun. Bearing in mind the fact that she's never seen the sea before, we were surprised when she began approaching the whitecaps that were gently breaking as they reached the beach. Penny seemed intrigued by them and then, she tentatively padded right up to the water's edge and dipped one of her front paws in the sea. Now, at any time of the year, the waters of the North Sea are definitely on the cold side, but Penny appeared unfazed by the water temperature as she slowly began to walk into the waves. Before we knew it, she was having the time of her life, jumping and splashing around in the sea. She wore a look of pure delight on her little face, and we laughed again as we saw how much she was enjoying herself. While this was taking place, Juliet walked Dylan closer to the water's edge, and tried to encourage him to have a paddle in the sea. There was more laughter as Dylan sort of dipped the end of one paw in the water, and then leaped back in shock, presumably from the cold temperature of the water, or maybe from the fact it was moving. Did he think it was some kind of giant monster?

Speaking of monsters, we now looked towards Penny, who was still in the sea, having a 'whale of a time,' (pardon the pun). She'd gone further out into the waves and for a moment, I was worried in case she got caught by the current and pulled out to sea. Suddenly, a larger wave approached the beach and for a few seconds, Penny disappeared beneath the white capped surf. Then, like a little sea monster rising from the deep, her head appeared, and, with a look of total enjoyment on her face, she powered her way up through the surf and headed towards us as we stood watching her in amazement. She was completely at home in the sea, and as she finally emerged, dripping from her swim in the ocean, she gave an almighty shake, soaking most of us, and wagged her tail which produced a constantly swerving spray of seawater as she shook out the sea from her rear appendage.

Sea monster!

"I think she's enjoyed that," Juliet said with a big smile on her face.

"I think you're right," I replied, "but we don't have a towel to dry her with, do we?"

We hadn't come prepared for either of the dogs to go swimming in the sea, so for the next half hour or so we carried on our walk in the afternoon sunshine, as Penny gradually dried off. Dylan, who'd eventually managed a sort of paddle in the shallowest of breaking waves, was hardly wet and his paws dried in no time.

By the time Penny had dried out, it was nearing the time for us to head for home, where my friend, Ken and our other dogs would be patiently awaiting our return. They'd all be wondering where we were. So, leaving the beach, and realising we were all hungry, we called at the nearest fish and chip shop, and bought ourselves some real seaside fish and chips, which we sat on the sea wall and ate, before heading to the car park. We were thankfully not bothered by any ravenous, roving seagulls as we ate, so were spared the sight of Dylan trying to take off into the Scarborough sky in his attempts to catch one.

I drove especially carefully on the way home, in an attempt to prevent a repeat of the morning journey, with Penny being sick during the ride. We had an idea that the movement was felt more violently in the rear of the car, so this time, we put Penny in the front foot well, between Juliet's feet, and, miraculously, it did the trick. The extra stability and security she felt must have helped to settle Penny's stomach, and of course, she was probably tired out by her oceanic exertions at the beach, so she slept most of the way home.

We were of course greeted like long lost best friends by the rest of the dogs on our return, and after feeding them all and saying thank you to Ken, who left for home, we were able to settle down together for the evening. All the dogs were soon snoozing peacefully, and Penny and Dylan were especially tired and were the first of the pack to be snoring happily., Dylan happily positioned, curled in a ball on my lap.

Our day at the seaside had been a happy and enjoyable one, and the mental picture of Penny, our very own sea monster, emerging triumphantly from the waves, lives with me to this day.

As for Dylan, neither Juliet nor I will ever forget his hilarious antics in trying to catch a seagull, nor the reaction of the people on the sea wall in applauding his efforts. His initial reluctance to enter the water and his subsequent enjoyment when he realised he could have some fun in the sea were yet another indication to us, that he was no longer that nervous and fearful little dog we'd met that first day at the sanctuary. At one point, he ventured so far out into the waves, that we were glad we'd kept him on his extending lead. I laughingly pointed my finger and called out to him, "Norway's that way, Dylan."

The photo collage that follows is a wonderful happy reminder to us of what was a fun-filled day at the beach for Dylan and Penny.

A day at the beach

10

DYLAN'S SPECIAL SQUIRREL

YOU MIGHT RECALL that at the end of an earlier chapter, I mentioned Dylan's fondness for soft toys, and that we'd return to that subject later. Okay, this is later, so it's time to tell the tale of Dylan's squirrel. Don't worry, it's not a real one, but it's an important part of Dylan's life so worthy of a mention in his story.

Before we get to his squirrel, however, it's best if I explain Dylan's attitude towards dog toys in general. When we first adopted him, he was so afraid of everything and everyone that even something as innocuous as a dog toy could scare him, if thrown towards him. The first toys he really played with were the teddy bears we bought him and Tilly, which I mentioned near the beginning of the book.

All pull together now!

Dylan and Tilly had great fun with their teddy bears and with almost anything soft on the mouth that they could play tug o' war with. Dylan has a very small mouth, and really can't get a good hold on most standard sized toys. Even a tennis ball, though soft, is a bit of a stretch for him. He will play with one, although he can't hold it in his mouth for long and will usually grab it and then drop it for someone to throw again for him.

In the early days we would give him small rubber bones to play with, but he never really showed much interest in them, appearing to become bored with them after a short time. We soon realised his small mouth and poor teeth combined probably contributed to his inability to derive much pleasure from regular toys, so we stuck with soft toys for him.

The only problem with this tactic was that most soft toys came with a built-in squeak. Within a pack of dogs, a squeaky toy is an instant signal for all-round mayhem, as every dog in the pack wants it, and whoever gets it usually destroys the squeaker within a few minutes. It's possible to buy squeak-less toys, but they tend to be expensive, and like all dog toys, have a very short life span, so they're really not worth the expense.

Over the years, we've probably spent a small fortune of doggie toys, and apart from a few, not many have stood the test of time. Once the squeaker in a dog toy was destroyed, it usually didn't take our pack very long to totally rip the toy to pieces, leaving us with a small pile of fabric that soon found its way into the bin.

The one exception to all the aforementioned mayhem and toy annihilation, was Dylan's squirrel. Now, don't let the dogs know about this, because this really is Dylan's very own 'Secret Squirrel.' This toy must be jealously guarded to protect it from the rest of our dogs, who would reduce it to shreds in minutes if they got hold of it.

I actually bought this little squirrel toy around nine, yes, *nine* years ago. It was originally meant to be shared by the smaller dogs in the pack, but it soon became evident to us that Dylan had a special liking for this particular toy. I jokingly said to Juliet,

"Maybe it reminds him of that day in the woods, when he was on the run for a couple of hours, happily chasing squirrels."

"Don't remind me of that day," she replied. "I still have nightmares thinking about what we'd have done if we hadn't been able to catch him."

"Doesn't bear thinking about," I agreed.

So, getting back to this little toy squirrel, it was a Christmas gift for our dogs. We've always bought a selection of toys and treats for our doggie family at Christmas. Doesn't everyone? Some of our dogs, (the brains of the pack), even know how to open their presents and wait until they're told to go ahead, before they proceed to tear the wrapping paper with their teeth, without damaging the contents.

Once opened, the fabric squirrel (not a plastic toy) was

immediately set upon by various sets of canine teeth, all eager to rip it to pieces! Sure enough, within half an hour of, shall we say, rough play, the squirrel had lost its squeak as had the squeaky duck and snake we'd bought them. We'd normally allow them to play with such toys for the rest of the day, and then, dispose of them the following morning, before we ended up with pieces of ravaged toys all over the house.

This time however, there was a difference. At bedtime, after we'd spent a happy and peaceful Christmas Day, we put the dogs out in the back garden last thing at night, and as we waited for them to drift back in to the house, Juliet and I went around the downstairs rooms picking up as much of the remains of chewed or broken dog toys, ready for disposal the next morning. Imagine my surprise therefore, to find Dylan already in his bed, curled up in a foetal position, with the squirrel tucked between his paws. He looked so cute, and I didn't have the heart to disturb him or attempt to remove the squirrel from between his front paws. I decided to leave him with the squirrel and sort it out in the morning.

When morning came around, however, I was surprised to discover that the squirrel hadn't been pulled apart or in any way destroyed. At some point during the previous day, Dylan must have 'rescued' it from the other dogs, and claimed it as his own, personal squirrel. I decided to take steps to make the toy safe from the other dogs whilst letting Dylan have the pleasure of playing with it. It wasn't as if he had any favourite or personal toys after all. Such things do tend to be difficult to achieve when living in a pack of dogs.

From that day forward, we kept the squirrel in a drawer in the utility room, only taking it out on occasions when Dylan could be allowed into the back garden on his own. Dylan loved these play sessions with his squirrel, which still go on today. He loves it when I throw it for him. He chases after it as it flies through the air and pounces on it as it lands and begins shaking it around as I've no doubt he would any rodent or small prey he caught in the wild. Watching him shake the poor thing around, I'm only glad he never actually caught a real live squirrel that day in the woods. It wouldn't have stood much chance of survival if Dylan had got his teeth into it.

He enjoys his play sessions and I take a lot of pleasure out of the time I spend with him, and his squirrel of course. When I think back to when we first met him and how I had to spend a month on the floor with him, teaching him to gradually trust and accept me, I'd never have thought back then that Dylan and I would now be so close as to be able to enjoy these little intimate moments together.

Get that squirrel, Dylan

ONE THING we discovered that Dylan loved, though we don't get it too often where we live, is...snow! I'm sure many dog owners out there would say the same. Most dogs seem to relish playing in snow, the deeper the better, and Dylan is no exception in that respect.

Because of the geographical lay of the land where we live, in the Vale of York, we are comparatively well sheltered from most extremes of weather. When the TV news is showing graphic shots of parts of the country being buried under deep snowfalls, with drifts often as much as six or seven feet deep, we are often completely clear of the white stuff!

The same goes for floods, which affect many areas of the country after particularly heavy downfalls, even as close as twenty miles from us. Recently, the news reported that we'd had the equivalent of a month's rainfall in twenty-four hours, bringing extensive flooding to many parts of the country. We received the rain, which was gratefully absorbed by our lawns and garden plants, but so effective is the land drainage in our area that we experienced no flooding at all.

But, back to the snow. I remember the first time Dylan woke up one morning and I opened the back door to let the dogs out. Juliet and I had already seen the snow when we opened our bedroom curtains and wondered how our little Beddie would react to it. Our other dogs, to the best of our knowledge had all experienced snow in the past, but we knew Dylan hadn't, so it would be interesting to see how he reacted to it.

The dogs drifted out into the garden in ones and twos as they usually did, and on feeling the snow beneath their paws, they were instantly on 'play alert' and without hesitation one or two began running around the garden, jumping and playing in the virgin snow.

Dylan, on the other hand, stood at the back door, ready to go out as usual to do his business and so on, and he 'froze' in place, excuse the pun. He was looking at the layer of soft white stuff that had fallen overnight, obliterating 'his' territory. As the other dogs were cheerfully going out and walking and running in this strange, alien substance, he tentatively took a couple of steps out of the door and his paws disappeared into the snow. He seemed unsure of himself (and the snow), at first, but then plucked up the courage to follow the others into the deeper snow further down the garden, away from the shelter of the house.

The next thing we saw was Dylan suddenly leaping around like a spring lamb, as he realised he could have some fun in this soft, white stuff. It was so funny to see him jumping and leaping and twisting in mid-air as he literally 'threw' himself into the fun to be had in the snow, and all this was before breakfast.

When the dogs came back inside, we had towels ready to give them a rub down and remove the snow from their paws. When Dylan decided he'd had enough of this new game, and came wandering back to the house, we discovered something new about Bedlington Terriers.

The fur of a Bedlington is actually a mix of rough and smooth fur, which gives it a 'linty' feel, but which also serves as a perfect snow trap. Poor Dylan had only been out in the snow for about five minutes, but his paws were already covered in balls of snow which had fixed themselves to his legs and tummy. Some of our other dogs had experienced this in the past but normally it took longer exposure to the snow to bring about such a covering of snowballs on their bodies. Juliet set to work with a fresh towel and was amazed that so much snow had attached itself to Dylan in so short a time, and the snow in our garden wasn't even particularly deep. It took her over ten minutes to gradually clear his legs and tummy of the frozen snow. It was important to make sure he was clear of ice which could cause frostbite and damage his legs.

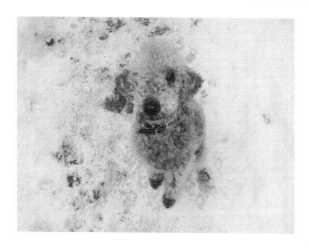

What's this white stuff, Dad?

"That's just the result of five minutes in the shallow snow in the garden," she said. "What's he going to look like after you take him with the others on the field to play, later?"

I pulled a face. "We can't really not let him go and enjoy himself with all the others, can we?" I replied.

"I know, but better not be too long on the field with them. We don't want the poor little mite getting frostbite."

I agreed and when Victoria and I took the 'gang' on the playing field later that morning, they all had a fantastic time, running and playing in the snow, but we made sure to limit the amount of time we allowed them for their 'winter sports'.

Snow racing

When we returned home it took us over half an hour to remove the frozen snowballs from their fur, with most of that time being taken up with Dylan. It was worth it though, when we saw how much fun he had, playing in the snow. It was a good job we kept a large supply of bath towels and bath sheets for our dogs; they certainly were well used over the three or four days the snow lay thickly on the ground. I don't think the washing machine and tumble dryer had been used so much for ages, and it was all dog towels!

Thankfully, as I said earlier, we very rarely experience snow, apart from the occasional flurry, but when we do, you can be sure the dogs thoroughly enjoy themselves, and we humans have to work hard to keep them clean, dry, and free from frozen ice balls.

11

SUN AND FUN

MOST DOGS LOVE THE SUN. I'm sure every dog owner reading this book knows that, but I've found over the years that some dogs love it more than others. The strangest thing about this sun-worshipping obsession is that I've found that dark-coloured dogs, whose colour attracts the sunlight more than light coloured canines, tend to be the biggest culprits. I use the word culprits deliberately, as I think you already know that too much time in the sun isn't good for your dog, but of course, it's definitely impossible to make a dog understand that too much time in the sun is bad for them.

The chief sun-worshippers in our family of dogs have been poor Dexter, who we lost in June of this year, and Muffin, who you've yet to meet in this story, but you won't have long to wait, and their colour...black!

Dexter, cooking nicely

Muffin wanting an all-over tan

Not far behind them is Dylan, who loves nothing more than being out in the garden with the sun on his back, snoozing in the heat of the day.

Happy Dylan

As long as the sun is shining our dogs are happy, and that's all we ever ask for them. Dylan, as the old man of the pack, could have been expected to slow down a little once he reached double figures, ten years old, but no, nothing seems to have put the brakes on his sense of enjoyment. He's always ready for a run and a game and still barks like a sabre-toothed wolf if he's approached by a strange, unknown dog. He's rediscovered his sense of fun when a tennis ball is thrown and will happily chase it and then, instead of bringing it back, or running with it, he'll simply lie on the grass with the ball in his mouth, attempting to chew it to pieces, which with Dylan's poor teeth isn't really a practical option for him. He usually ends up doing a few roly-polys ending up lying on his back with the ball still firmly grasped in his teeth. Because he has such a small mouth and as you'll see in the photo below, Dylan can't actually get a tennis ball fully into his mouth like other dogs but is quite happy grasping it in one side of his jaws. Once that ball is in his grasp, he won't give it up and will resist any attempt by me, Victoria or anyone to remove it from his mouth. Big tough

Dylan will only drop that ball when he's good and ready to do so.

Do I look tough?

Juliet and I were discussing Dylan's small mouth one day after having watched the movie, *Jaws II* on DVD the previous evening. I don't know how the subject came up in our conversation, but, if you've seen the movie, you might recall the scene where a dead killer whale is washed up on the beach and Chief Brody (*Roy Scheider*), convinced it's a victim of a great white shark, asks a marine scientist, played by actress *Collin Wilcox* to measure the bit radius of whatever creature killed the whale. Somehow, this scene had lingered in my mind and I jokingly said to Juliet,

"You know, if we think of Sheba, with her wide staffy

mouth, as the great white, then by comparison, Dylan probably has the bite radius of a newt."

She couldn't help laughing at my comparison.

"Aw, poor Dylan," she said reaching out to give him a sympathetic stroke. "Your dad thinks you're a newt."

As Dylan hadn't the faintest idea what we were talking about, he just stood there, enjoying the attention and wagging his tail. Now we're on the subject let's stay with Dylan's teeth.

Three years had passed since Dylan had undergone his veterinary teeth cleaning procedure, and when I took him for his annual booster vaccination, the vet gave him a clean bill of health, apart from his teeth...again!

Although I was reluctant to pay over a hundred pounds yet again, the vet convinced me to have the procedure carried out again as, even though it might not result in a prefect set of pearly-whites, it might if nothing else, prolong the life of Dylan's teeth and perhaps save him from future pain which might lead to him needing his teeth taking out.

When we got home from the vet, I talked it over with Juliet and we agreed to go ahead and let the vet clean them once again. I duly phoned the vet the next day and booked Dylan in for the following week.

Showing off his nice clean teeth!

We had to admit, that after this second cleaning procedure, his teeth looked even better than after the first time we'd had it done. As usual though, over time, his gnashers would revert to their usual yellow appearance, as the plaque built up again.

YOU HAVE WON *second prize in a beauty competition.* No, we weren't playing a game of Monopoly, but were at the annual 'Scruffs' Dog Show, which was organised and held at the sanctuary where we'd found Dylan, and so many of our other dogs. I'm sure many of you dog owners have attended similar events with your own dogs, and perhaps taken part of some of the fun activities and entered your dogs in some of the various show groups, *Dog with the waggiest tail,* or *Dog with the best smile, Best Rescue Dog, Best senior dog* and so on.

We'd decided to attend the event again one year and decided to take Dylan along so Jennie and the sanctuary staff could see what a beautiful dog he'd turned into, a far cry from the poor, terrified, scruffy little Beddie we'd first seen on his first day at the sanctuary. You might recall we'd attended a previous show and didn't enter Dylan in any of the groups because he was still quite a nervous dog at the time. This time was different.

We arrived good and early on the day of the event so we could have a good look round at the various stalls and the goods on offer. There were lots of owners and their dogs present, obviously and we had quite a few conversations with people who were interested in Dylan. Bedlington Terriers, despite their relative popularity, are still very much an unknown quantity to many dog owners and we were happy to explain to those who asked, as much as we could about the breed and its history. Most people were surprised to hear they were originally bred as hunting dogs, and looking at a Beddie, it's easy to see why.

We reached the stand where entries for the show were being taken, and after we'd had a good look at the various 'classes' to be judged, we entered Dylan into the 'Best Rescue Dog' category, and had an hour to wait before he would be 'on show'.

The judging began soon afterwards, and two categories took place before Dylan's turn eventually arrived. Victoria was keen to lead him round the show ring and as Dylan always behaved well for her, we agreed to her request. She looked so proud as she put him through his paces, walking nicely round the show ring, stopping and sitting perfectly when she instructed him to do so, allowing the judge to pet him and take a close look at him, at the same time asking Victoria some questions about his history etc. Victoria did really well, answering all her questions without hesitation. When the judge had looked at all the dogs in the category, about twenty I think, everyone stood and waited expectantly for the result to be announced.

Dylan was awarded second place! Victoria proudly led him to the centre of the ring, where the judge presented Dylan with a rosette and a bag of treats, which Victoria received on his behalf of course. Although we'd have loved him to come first, second place was still terrific and Victoria was over the moon as she came over to us, and I pinned the rosette to his collar. For the rest of the afternoon, Dylan strutted around the grounds proudly displaying his rosette, and Victoria couldn't wait to tell all her friends at school about it the following day.

There was an official photographer present, organised by the sanctuary, who took photographs of all the winners and runners-up in the various categories, with the option to buy the photos being offered to the participants. They weren't cheap, of course; these things never are, but Victoria begged us to buy a copy of Dylan's photo, and we agreed, as it would make a nice souvenir of Dylan's day at 'Scruffs'.

We stayed to watch a few more of the categories being judged, but time seemed to fly by and before we knew it, the time came when we had to say goodbye to our friends at the sanctuary and make our way home, where our other dogs would be patiently awaiting our return. It would be their feeding time by the time we arrived, so we were assured of an excited welcome home!

Dylan and his rosette

12

NEW FACES

THE YEARS WERE FLYING PAST, or so it seemed, and the one constant through all the changes that were taking place was...Dylan. As our family underwent comings and goings, our little Beddie was always around, not always to the forefront of what was happening, but definitely in the background.

Perhaps the biggest change that occurred within our little pack of rescues was the addition of a little staffy who joined us almost nine years ago, and who has gone on to achieve 'star status' among our dogs. I refer of course ... to Sasha!

Abandoned in a gutter at about 5 weeks old, almost dead from hypothermia when found and picked up by a dog warden, she joined our family at 7 weeks of age, and has lived an amazing life so far. Two broken legs, skin allergies, canine epilepsy which first manifested itself when she was only two years old, her story, told in book one of this series, Sasha, has gone on to become an international bestseller, as Sasha, through her own Facebook page has gone on to recruit a legion of fans around the world, until she has become kind of icon for epileptic dogs everywhere.

As I sit writing this chapter, she's undergoing tests for Addison's Disease, but whatever befalls her, this wonderful little girl seems to bounce back from whatever life throws at her.

New puppy

When she first arrived in our home, Sasha was so tiny, we couldn't find a dog collar small enough to fit her, so we had to use a very small pale blue cat collar, with a bell attached, and even that was enormous on her. At least, with the bell, we could hear her coming or find her as wandered around the house. All the dogs, Dylan included, immediately welcomed the tiny puppy into our home and family, and Sasha, with all the typical inquisitiveness of a puppy, enjoyed exploring her new home and surroundings.

After she'd been with us a couple of weeks, at no more than ten weeks old, she was playing on the landing with Dinky, as I was getting dressed, when she suddenly disappeared through a small gap between the stair rail and the bannister, and fell straight down to the hallway below. I dashed down the stairs to find our beautiful little puppy lying dazed on the floor, with one front leg sticking out at an unnatural angle. Juliet, arrived home, having been out for a walk with three of the dogs, we both realised Sasha was seriously hurt.

Neither of us had even imagined a dog, even one as small as Sasha could have slipped through that gap, but it was no time for inquests. I phoned the vet, explained the situation and was told to take her to the surgery right away. Juliet found an old wicker shopping basket she'd had since her schooldays, and quickly lined it with a blanket. She carried little Sasha out to the car, and placed her on the front seat, her injured leg sticking out over the edge of the basket. Poor little pup hadn't made a sound since the fall. She was being incredibly brave.

The vet immediately took her through for x-rays and it wasn't long before they told me Sasha had a broken elbow joint and would require an operation to fix it. Thankfully, we'd received six weeks free insurance from the dog pound when we adopted Sasha, otherwise we'd never have been able to afford the cost of the operation and poor Sasha wouldn't have been here today. Sasha was kept at the surgery and as luck would have it, the orthopaedic surgeon was due to visit that very day, so there was no delay in her receiving the required treatment. The surgeon later told me he'd had to insert a metal plate, bolts and screws in her joint and Sasha would have to spend three months in a crate, resting as much as possible, only being allowed out to go to the toilet and for gentle exercise, a few minutes each day.

Sasha would spend the next three months in a medium size dog crate and the poor little mite looked so forlorn in there. I spent nearly the whole time sitting beside her in a garden chair so she wouldn't get lonely. Perhaps that's where the incredible bond that exists between Sasha and me was born. Dylan and the other dogs would come and look at her in the crate, probably wondering why she was locked away and only allowed out for short periods. When I did take her out in the garden, the little puppy would still try to play with the other dogs, and I had to stop her from doing too much. Even at that early age, Sasha was no problem when it came to taking medication and took her painkillers without any fuss.

Eventually, she was given the all clear by the surgeon. Sasha could be a 'real' puppy at last. She loved it, being able to run and play with the other dogs, in the garden and on the playing field when she joined them for longer walks. Everyone who met her commented on what a beautiful little dog she was, and it was just so good to see her happy and enjoying life at last.

Unfortunately, disaster lay just around the corner. After just two weeks of running free and having a great time, one day, Sasha tried to jump over the baby gate that separated the kitchen from the utility room. Sadly, she somehow mistimed her jump, because, as she went over the gate, she caught it with her trailing legs, and went down heavily on her front legs, breaking the same elbow joint that had just healed!

The orthopaedic surgeon could hardly believe it. He told me that he'd never known a dog so young break the same joint in the same place in such a short space of time. Sasha would need another operation to repair her leg, and due to the fact she'd grown considerably since the first break, the surgeon would have to completely remove the nuts, bolts plate he'd previously inserted and fashion new ones for her by now severely damaged elbow.

Poor Sasha. I felt so sad and sorry for her. After already been stuck in a crate for three months of her puppyhood, and only having had two weeks since her recovery to enjoy being a puppy again, she was faced with going through it all again. Yet, despite all her problems, Sasha's tail never stopped wagging. She was always happy.

Cuddles after her second operation

* * *

FINALLY, after another three months convalescence, Sasha got the all clear once again, and she was free to run and play, and make up for lost time. The other dogs welcomed her into their midst once more and Sasha threw herself into enjoying being a puppy!

One dog, however, wasn't quite so welcoming. Despite having gone through so much, Sasha was her usual exuberant self once she'd been given the all clear to resume normal life. Always a happy little soul, with her tail wagging non-stop, she'd walk around the house or garden busily greeting the other dogs in turn. When it came to Dylan, her tail wagged so much her entire rear end wiggled with it. She was obviously so pleased to see Dylan and wanted to be friends with him. But, for some reason, Dylan wouldn't acknowledge her. The more she wagged her tail at him, the more he ignored her, until he grew fed up with her attempts to befriend him, he barked at her. Now, Dylan's bark isn't what you could describe as particularly threatening, and Sasha just ignored his adverse reaction to her greeting and wagged her tail even more. He barked some more, and she wagged some more, and so it went on. Eventually we had to force little Sasha to come away and leave him alone.

"Come away, Sasha," I told her. "Grumpy-Chops doesn't want to know you. Leave him alone and go and play with the others."

Of course, being a puppy, albeit a rather big one now after having spent so much of her first year locked in a crate, Sasha was happy as long as she had someone to play with and there was no shortage of play pals in our house, that's for sure.

As time went on however, this strange behaviour from Dylan showed no sign of abating, and to this day, Sasha will do everything she can to get Dylan to like her, and all he does is bark at her. In a way, it's funny to see, but it's also quite heart-breaking, because Sasha obviously loves Dylan and would probably love nothing more than to cuddle up with him, but he just doesn't want anything to do with her. It's like a case of unrequited canine love and silly old Dylan isn't interested in the gorgeous Sasha. No wonder we jokingly call him *Victor Meldrew*, (a famous character in a British TV sitcom, known for his grumpy behaviour and his favourite phrase, 'Oh my God, you cannot be serious').

If Dylan didn't want anything to do with Sasha, how would he react when three more puppies arrived on the scene, soon after Sasha's second birthday? Petal, Muffin and Digby are two sisters and their brother, all adopted by us in response to an advertisement in the local paper.

Juliet had been feeling quite depressed after the loss of one of our dogs, and though we know you can't just replace a dog that held a place in your heart, I knew from experience that if she had a new puppy to take care of, it would give her a new focus and help to take her mind off the loss of Chudleigh, her special pup. I'd told her to keep an eye on the local press for any puppies being offered for sale and one day she pointed out an advert that had caught her eye. A litter of pups was being offered for sale, advertised as Springer Spaniel/Staffy crosses. The advert said that both parents could be seen, always a good point, so I phoned up the number in the ad and made arrangements for Juliet and me to go to see them the following day.

To cut a long story short, we ended up taking not one, but two of the puppies and three weeks later, a third, when Digby joined Muffin and Petal as the latest additions to our canine family.

Dylan accepted the puppies as soon as we brought them into the house. Obviously, being little babies, he could tell they were no threat to him, and he basically left them alone, having very little to do with them.

Not so Sasha, who now proceeded to amaze us. Within two hours of little Muffin and Petal arriving in our house, having run around the garden and house, getting to know all the dogs, they were obviously tired out and Juliet picked them up, and placed them in one of the beds in the kitchen. A few minutes later I called out to her,

"Juliet, come and take a look at this."

She came into the kitchen and there were the two puppies curled up fast asleep, being watched over and looked after... by Sasha!

Sasha had taken the role of surrogate mother to the pups, and from that first day, she made it her responsibility to guide and educate the puppies, who followed her everywhere. We hardly had to do any house training, because when Sasha went out to garden, the puppies dutifully followed her and soon learned the art of 'telling' us when the needed to go to the toilet. I can honestly say that those puppies never once did a wee or a poo in the house, quite incredible! They were no trouble at all and when their brother Digby joined us three weeks later, Sasha again took him under her wing, and he was trained in no time, like his sisters. We concluded that Sasha must have very strong, natural maternal instincts, because she'd never had pups of her own, and had been spayed at nine months old, so had no actual experience of caring for puppies. It all came naturally, and some years later, she would do the same again when another puppy, Honey, joined the family.

Sasha with baby Muffin & Petal

As soon as they were old enough and had been fully inoculated, we started taking the three puppies for walks on the nearby large playing field where they had space to play and to investigate the small copses of bushes and trees that were planted around the field. They were so well behaved. It seemed as if Sasha had somehow instilled in their little minds exactly what they could and couldn't do. It became something of a joke within the family that having the puppies was like having one dog with twelve legs, as whatever one did, or wherever one went, the others did exactly the same thing.

So, our pack of rescue dogs was growing and changing as time passed. Our little family was by now very different from the days when Dylan and Tilly came to us, joining Sophie and Candy in our home and our lives. No matter who came and went however, Dylan just kept on going in the same way, happily going about his life with scant concern for anything that may have been going on around him.

Muffin, Digby and Petal, 10 weeks old

We decided our Dylan was something of an aristocrat among dogs, rather posh and almost looking down his nose at the commoners below him! He's always had a kind of superior air about him. He walks so proudly, almost on tiptoes, so he appears to be prancing along like a show pony, his tail held straight and proud behind him.

A handsome chap!

He still loved his walks of course of nothing pleased him more than going to the smaller of our two playing fields where he could enjoy a run and play. Rebecca would often take him to play with his ball, and the pair of them would enjoy a particularly warm and sunny summer as almost permanent play partners. Dylan loved his time with her and would always come home with a spring in his step, and his tongue lolling out to one side, a sure sign he'd had a great time.

Fun on the field with Rebecca

People will often stop us while out for our walks and want to pet him. There's something about a Beddie that attracts people to them, doubtless their lamb-like appearance. Many people know what he is of course, though a large number have no idea. A lot of people think he's a poodle. I'm sure *Dylan* would have something to say about that!

Another thing that fools people is his age. Due to the abuse and malnutrition he suffered in his first year of life, Dylan has never grown to the usual size of a full-grown Bedlington and this has probably contributed to people thinking he's still a young dog. Of course, his general fitness helps to maintain that illusion of youth and they always express surprise when I tell them he's over ten years old.

One thing I encourage people to do is to stroke Dylan briskly on his back, between his back legs. This is obviously a very sensitive point on Dylan's body and doing this makes him indulge in the 'Dylan dance'. Everyone loves to see it as he lifts his back legs in turn as if he really is dancing. He seems to know it amuses people and will sometimes carry on the 'dance' for a few seconds even after the stroking has stopped. He looks as if he enjoys it, otherwise I wouldn't let him do it. It certainly gets his tail wagging. People see him 'dancing' and they just fall in love with him.

But of course, it's very easy to fall in love with a Beddie!

13

A STROKE FOR DYLAN

IF YOU'VE READ Sasha's story, the first book in this series, you'll know that at the age of two, she developed canine epilepsy, and has battled this invidious disease ever since, with great fortitude and bravery. In a couple of months, she'll reach her ninth birthday, a landmark we weren't confident she'd make in the early days, when she'd suffer regular 'cluster fits', three or four seizures one after the other, every month. Over time, and with tweaks and changes to her medications, the epilepsy is now more controlled than in those early years, but it's always upsetting to see your dog going through a seizure even though they don't know it's happening to them, and the aftermath, the recovery phase is far more uncomfortable for them, as they can be uncoordinated, wobbly on their legs, (Sasha certainly is), and just 'not themselves' often for a day or two.

My reason for mentioning Sasha's problems at this point is to illustrate that over the years, Juliet and I have become used to dealing with the needs of a disabled or 'special needs' dog, as Sasha has to follow a strict diet and there are a whole host of do's and don'ts attached to her daily existence. We don't really notice them anymore because they're ingrained in our daily routine. You'll see why I've talked about this soon.

Having reached the age of 11 years, Dylan was still super-fit, apart from his grotty teeth, which the vet always tried to get us to have cleaned again, (another £150), to which I said a polite, "No thank you."

Every time we've had them done, it only takes a few months for the plaque to build up again and make the procedure seem to be a total waste of time. This time however, when we went for his annual booster, we met a new vet at the practice. Ximo, (pronounced Cheemo), is Spanish, and if you've read *Remembering Dexter,* you'll have heard of him already.

As usual, in addition to giving Dylan his annual booster, he examined him thoroughly, effectively giving Dylan a brief MOT check. For readers not from the UK an MOT test is something all cars over three years old must undergo each year, by law, to ensure they are fit to be on the road. He checked all Dylan's vital signs, heart lungs etc and then he came to his mouth...and those teeth.

"His teeth are not very good," Ximo said, as if I didn't know.

"They've been like that since we got him," I replied, and went on to relate Dylan's awful treatment as a puppy to Ximo, who nodded and instantly seemed to understand just why Dylan's teeth were so prone to the build-up of plaque. It seems Dylan probably suffered as a puppy from extreme vitamin deficiencies which affected the growth of his teeth, leaving them lacking in certain essential parts of their make-up. Also, his mouth being so narrow meant that his saliva didn't drain as efficiently as it should, all of which led to the poor state of his teeth. In other words, we could spend money on having them cleaned until the sun fell from the sky and it wouldn't make any difference. He'd always have exactly the teeth he'd always had. At least that was one thing we shouldn't need to concern ourselves with in the future, which was just as well, as you'll soon discover.

Winter came around once more and it was an extremely mild one. No snow, but some bitterly cold and freezing days, especially in the mornings, with frost and ice covering the ground in a white blanket, which was almost as bad, if not worse than a heavy snowfall. At least, after the snow settled, us humans weren't slipping and sliding on the ice. It's not always easy trying to keep your feet when you have three dogs on leads, wanting to rush off in different directions.

Dylan has had a nice, dark blue dog coat almost since the day we got him. It's a very good quality coat, and we've never had one last so long for any of our dogs. The only drawback is that it's not especially warm for him now that he's a senior citizen, so, I went shopping one day and bought some nice dog sweaters, for those of our dogs we felt would benefit from them on icy morning walks. It amused to buy one for Dylan with a penguin on it. Penguins after all, have quite a distinctive appearance, rather like Dylan does.

Dylan's penguin coat

Thankfully, time seemed to fly, and it wasn't long before the crocuses and snowdrops were in full bloom and the daffodils were doing their best to push their way towards to sun. Spring was rushing to replace winter and bring a little colour and cheer to the gardens.

One morning, we rose early as usual and while Juliet put the kettle on for her morning tea, (and my coffee), I unlocked the back door to let the dogs out as I always did. As was normal, some went straight away, some waited a few minutes and then wandered out to do what they needed to do.

A short time later, I looked around as I sipped my coffee and thought it unusual that Dylan hadn't come in. He'd usually come back into the house and then, when it was time for breakfast, he'd make his way outside again, as he liked his breakfast outside for some reason. He'd always preferred it that way, probably some kind of throwback to when he was a puppy, and maybe had to fight for his food, what there was of it.

"Where's Dylan?" I wondered, and Juliet, like me hadn't seen him since he went out. "I'll go and get him," I said, as I went out into the garden.

I saw him straight away. He was wandering around like a drunk, his legs seemingly uncoordinated and he was staggering, and unresponsive when I spoke to him. I called Juliet, who came out to join me and immediately agreed there was something wrong. I didn't want to take him indoors in case any of the other dogs reacted aggressively to his strange behaviour, so I left him there, went in to make myself another cup of coffee, and then returned to the garden to watch over him. His strange behaviour continued for another five minutes or so, and then he just lay down on the ground, and seemed to be sleeping. I couldn't leave him like that, and as he was apparently asleep, I picked him up and carried him indoors and placed him gently in his bed.

"What do you think?" Juliet asked, once we were sure he was settled down.

"Well, we know it wasn't an epileptic fit," I replied. We'd been through enough seizures with Sasha over the years to be able to recognise an epileptic fit when we saw one, and this definitely didn't resemble any epileptic seizure we'd ever seen. "As soon as the vet opens, I'll take him straight down there. We need to know what it is."

An hour or so later, at 8.15, I phoned the veterinary surgery, gave them a brief description of Dylan's symptoms, and they agreed I should take him in straight away. Dylan was quite lucid by now, and was able to walk with me, on his lead, to the car, where he jumped up into the back as normal. To all intents and purposes, it was as if nothing had happened, but we knew otherwise, and it was important to have him checked out.

Sure enough, the vets treated it seriously and Dylan and I were shown straight through to a consultation room on our arrival. Rebecca, the senior partner at the practice was the attending vet and after giving Dylan a thorough examination he made his diagnosis.

"From the symptoms you've described to me, Brian, I'm pretty sure that Dylan's had a small stroke."

I was stunned. This was our super fit; never had a day's illness Dylan we were talking about.

"That's bad news," I said, not really knowing what to say. "Are you sure?"

"Pretty much. The other possibility is IVD, that's idiopathic vestibular disease but in Dylan's case I think he's had a slight ischaemic stroke. That'd when there's a sudden lack of blood supply to the brain. The other type of stroke in dogs is haemorrhagic stroke, and that happens when there's bleeding within the brain, which I'm sure isn't the case here, or Dylan wouldn't be up and about so soon and behaving normally. I'd like to do some blood tests to be certain if you don't mind?"

"Go ahead," I said. "Let's do whatever's necessary to help him."

Rebecca took Dylan through to the treatment rooms for a few minutes and soon returned with him, blood samples taken. I was allowed to take Dylan home with instructions to keep him as quiet as possible for a day or two after which he should be back to normal.

Sure enough, the tests later confirmed that Dylan had suffered an ischaemic stroke. Rebecca explained that although dogs do suffer from strokes, they're usually not as serious as their human equivalent, and Dylan should make a full recovery.

As suggested, we kept Dylan as quiet as possible for the next few days and during that time he exhibited no further symptoms, and we allowed him to return to normal activities, though for some time afterwards both Juliet and I tended to always watch him closely when he was outside in the garden, just in case! Dylan, as the senior member of our doggie family is after all, very special to us.

A very special boy

14

___

VISION IMPAIRED, CAN YOU HEAR ME?

DYLAN'S STROKE was soon virtually forgotten as he appeared to shrug it off and continued as usual, living life to the full. With all the changes that had taken place in our doggie family over the years, it was remarkable that he never seemed put out or upset at the number of alterations to his routine that had to be made in order to cope with the assimilation of the new members of the family.

Perhaps the most notable change was in the make-up of his walking partners over the last two years. You may recall me mentioning his attitude towards Sasha, who without a doubt loves Dylan, while Dylan would appear to hate Sasha. Maybe that's too strong a word, but he certainly doesn't reciprocate her feelings towards him.

Juliet now walks the faster, more energetic dogs, while I'm in charge of the slower and older dogs. My own health problems mean I can't go running and playing with the dogs on the field any longer so I'm in charge of 'the old crocks brigade' as we refer to them.

Although Dylan is still fast and agile, the next visit to the vet for his annual booster vaccination, following his stroke, brought a new problem to light. Approximately six months had passed since the stroke and Dylan was doing great, still as fit and healthy as ever, when his booster became due.

We arrived at the vets in advance of his allotted appointment time, and the staff in reception made a really big fuss of him. Thought they didn't see him very often, they all knew who he was, and took advantage of him being there by giving him lots of hugs and cuddles, which Dylan loved of course. He's a real love bug, always has been and he'd have happily accepted their attention all day if I'd let him.

Our turn came around and we were called into the consulting room by the vet. He was pleased to see Dylan doing so well and his routine examination revealed no new problems, until... he was looking directly at Dylan, and he had an odd look on his face. I said nothing, as he was clearly checking for something. When he straightened up, the vet said,

"Brian, did you know Dylan has a slight problem with his vision?"

"I haven't noticed anything," I replied.

"He has the beginnings of cataracts," he said, "and he possibly has something called nuclear sclerosis. That's a condition usually associated with age and isn't dangerous and doesn't require any treatment."

"So, what do we do?" I asked, thinking our beautiful boy was about to go blind overnight.

"Nothing," was the reply. "The cataracts aren't very well developed and even if they were, I wouldn't recommend Dylan as a good candidate for surgery."

It seemed that poor Dylan, having always been so fit and healthy, was beginning to develop some age-related problems, but I agreed with the decision not to recommend surgery.

Dylan was still happy and healthy and after his stroke, I didn't think surgery would be a good idea.

When we got him and I told Juliet, she was totally in agreement that we didn't want Dylan to undergo surgery at his age. He was now thirteen years old and we didn't want to take any chances with his health.

His new condition did, however, lead to him being placed in the 'old codgers' group for walks and we had to make certain adjustments to our walking routine. From that day, Dylan would share his morning walk with his arch nemesis, Sasha, and Sheba, also by then one of our seniors, and who was suffering with arthritis in her leg joints, and who consequently walked much slower than she had done previously.

Sasha went for two walks in the mornings, having earlier walked with Petal and Penny. She would then not go out in the afternoon, by which time her large cocktail of medications made her quite sleepy in the afternoons.

Dylan's afternoon walks were now shared with Sheba and Muttley, so he had two staffies for companies on both of his daily walks. As he walked with me and his staffy 'escorts' there was no way anyone would have guessed he had a problem with his vision.

The odd thing about Dylan's new walking routine, bearing in mind his relationship, (or should it be non-relationship) with Sasha, was that while they were out walking together, it appeared that Dylan had put hostilities on hold. Up to this day, whenever he's out walking with Sasha, Dylan behaves like a perfect gentleman towards her, and I can tell how happy Sasha is as she walks along beside him, happily wagging her tail.

Dylan, Sasha & Sheba stop for a treat

Everything was going well, and Dylan's slight vision problem was all but forgotten as he showed no sign of having any difficulty seeing where he was going, and it wasn't as if he walked around the house bumping into things. So, the months went by and we almost forgot he had a problem.

The only time the subject came up was when Juliet had him on the grooming table for his regular session and she always made sure she clipped his head nicely and made sure his fur was clear of his eyes.

A kiss for Mum after grooming

It was round about this time that Dylan began to show the first physical signs of ageing. It wasn't much, but Juliet and I both noticed small areas of his fur were changing from his beautiful Bedlington Blue to a dirty-looking pale brown. Our other dogs turned grey as they aged, Dylan it would appear, turned brown!

So far, it's not especially noticeable to most people, but we can see it, in small patches round his mouth and feet. Let's hope it doesn't spread too much, or we might end up with a brown Bedlington. Thankfully, Juliet, who by the way had taken and passed a dog grooming course some years ago, is skilled enough to mask most of Dylan's 'brown bits' by clever snipping and grooming with her 'magic' grooming scissors.

Dylan's slight colour changes are really *very* slight by comparison with poor Sheba, who around the same time seemed to age very quickly. Though her body still retains its beautiful brindle colour, her head and face began to turn grey virtually overnight and in the ensuing months the ageing process continued until today her head and face are virtually white.

Some dogs seem to age more than others and of course, the luckiest dogs are the white ones. They don't seem to age at all. Penny is fifteen and shows no sign of ageing, nor does Sasha, although she won't be nine until December, and Petal, at seven is too young to show any signs of age. In Penny's case, perhaps because of the white fur mixed in with the black on her face, she's always looked older than her years. When we first adopted her and took her for her first few walks, all our dog-owning friends thought we'd adopted a little old dog, and we had to correct them, explaining that Penny was only about 18 months old. She's never changed, so it's perhaps not surprising that she doesn't seem to have aged, she's always looked the same!

Penny, growing old gracefully

Cassie is fifteen too and incredibly she shows no signs of

growing old either in attitude, behaviour, or colour. Our little 'mad ferret' Duracell bunny just goes on and on and on, completely impervious to the ageing gene, so it seems.

Sheba twelve years ago

Sheba 18 July 2019

Sheba today

* * *

ONE DAY, during the summer, the dogs were all in the back garden lounging in the sunshine, as dogs love to do, as the time for afternoon walks crept up on us. It was time for Dylan to go for his walk with Sheba and Muttley. One shout of each name was usually enough for all three to come running into the house, ready to have their leads on and to go for their walk. Sure enough, Sheba and Muttley were by my side almost immediately, sitting nicely as we waited for Dylan to join us. When he didn't appear us usual, I looked out of the utility room window to see him still lying on one of the outdoor beds we put out for the dogs during the summer, presumably still snoozing and enjoying the sun.

I called him again, but still received no response. Leaving

Sheba and Muttley looking mystified, sitting with their leads on, I went out to the garden to try and hurry Dylan up. When I reached him, he was contentedly lying there, enjoying the warmth of the sun.

"Come on, mate. It's time for walkies," I said, and Dylan ignored me. "Dylan, come on, get up little fella," and Dylan lifted his head. I had his lead in my hand and as soon as he saw it, he jumped up and bounded up and down with his usual excitement at going for his walk.

I clipped his lead on and went and collected Sheba and Muttley and we carried on with our afternoon walk without further incident. Later, when I returned from the walk, I spoke with Juliet.

"Dylan was weird when I went out to get him," I told her. "It was like he was ignoring me, which isn't like Dylan, or he just couldn't hear me."

"Oh, don't tell me he's going deaf as well as blind," she replied.

We went to where Dylan was once again lounging in the garden. I took a few biscuits with me in case we needed to attract his attention.

"Dylan," Juliet said, and he looked up straight away. "He heard that," she said, and I nodded my agreement.

"Maybe it's the tone of your voice," I replied. "It's a higher pitch than mine."

"He's an old man now, maybe he's just a bit hard of hearing," she suggested.

"What? Like me? I joked. I must admit, I'm sometimes a bit on the deaf side. I find it difficult to hear individuals when I'm in a room full of people or even if the TV is playing in the same room. Maybe Dylan had a similar problem.

We decided to leave things as they were for a while and see how Dylan reacted to us over the next few weeks. Over the next three weeks we couldn't help but notice that Dylan definitely had a hearing problem, unless, like some elderly people I know, he was suffering from what I call 'selective deafness' and tuning out when he couldn't be bothered with what we had to say.

Finally, it reached a point where, when we were out for a walk and I stopped to give the dogs a treat, Sasha and Sheba, or Muttley, depending on whether it was his morning or afternoon walk, would instantly stop and look up in anticipation of their treat. Dylan would stop of course, he had no option, but he didn't look up, and when I'd speak, saying, "Who wants a biscuit?" the other dogs would instantly react, but Dylan just stared straight ahead or looked around at the passing cars, or other pedestrians. It was obvious he couldn't hear me. As a kind of experiment, the next time we stopped, I spoke to him again, for quite a long time without getting a reaction from him, but when I gently tapped him with a finger on the top of his head, he instantly looked up and took notice of me. That confirmed it, Dylan was going deaf.

As there's no cure for deafness, and as far as I know, there are no hearing aids for dogs, we decided it wasn't worth another vet visit for Dylan. After all, the worst they could tell us was that he was going deaf, and we knew that already!

Showing his age, still a stunning looker though

15

DRUNK AGAIN DYLAN? IS THAT A NEW PUPPY DAD?

A FEW WEEKS LATER, Dylan was drunk again; in other words, our gorgeous little fella suffered a second stroke. I'd recently returned from our morning walk, with Dylan as usual accompanied by Sasha and Sheba. Everything was fine until Dylan went out in the back garden. As I looked out of the window, I saw him cock his leg up to do a wee, next to the garden shed. He did what he had to do and as he walked away, I saw him stagger slightly, and then walk around the garden looking dazed, as though he was about to fall over any minute. The episode lasted no more than a minute and if I hadn't been watching through the window, I might never have known it had taken place.

I called Juliet and together we went outside and examined him closely. There were no visible signs of any injury, no thorns in his pads or anything we could see that might have caused him pain in his legs and make him stagger.

We watched him closely for the rest of the day, but he showed no further symptoms and was his usual bouncy self again within half an hour of the episode. I rang the vet who, after listening to my explanation of what had taken place, said that, in all probability, Dylan had suffered another minor stroke, but if he was behaving perfectly normal, there didn't seem much point in me taking him to the surgery.

He explained once again that strokes in dogs tend to differ greatly from those in human beings and that in general, they are not as serious, unless of course they are of the haemorrhagic variety of stroke, which were caused by bleeding in the brain, and it was pretty much certain that wasn't applicable in Dylan's case. We were advised to watch him closely and report any further symptoms to the surgery.

I'm please to say that since that day, around eighteen months ago, there have been no further stroke-like episodes, and Dylan has remained perfectly healthy, apart from his deafness and sight problems.

Speak up, I'm a little hard of hearing!

* * *

AT THE AGE OF FIFTEEN, Dylan remains one of the fittest dogs in our rescue family. No two dogs are the same of course, but when we compare him with, say, Sheba, (13) and Penny, (also

15), both of whom have slowed down considerably due to arthritis, he really is quite remarkable.

He still loves to run and play, bounding around in the back garden like a spring lamb, and of course, he loves to play with his squirrel, (yes, it's still going strong and in one piece after all these years). How on earth that toy has lasted so long makes the mind boggle. As long as Dylan has fun with it, it'll remain in the drawer where it lives in the utility room, to be taken out and 'savaged' by our bouncing Beddie whenever he's in playful mode.

"Hey, Dad, there's a dog inside that telly thing."

A LITTLE UNDER two years ago, Dylan was faced with a new playmate. Victoria, by now all grown up and working for a living, was constantly asking if we could get a new puppy. Both Juliet and I repeatedly told her that we didn't want any more dogs. With Sasha, Sheba, Penny and Dylan all having health issues, and needing extra care, we didn't want to add more paws to care for. As things turned out, our words fell on deaf ears, (not Dylan's either).

One evening, two weeks before Christmas, Victoria was a

little late getting home from work. She often went to see friends before coming home so we weren't unduly concerned by her late arrival. We'd done all our afternoon dog walks, fed all the dogs, and given medications to those that required them, and then settled down in the lounge, surrounded by the dogs of course. We usually managed to sit down for an hour between 6 and 7 in the evening, relaxing and watching TV for a while before having to start preparing our evening meal.

Shortly after six o'clock, we heard Victoria coming in through the front door. She asked her mum to go outside with her and Juliet immediately thought something bad had happened and asked her why. Victoria simply repeated that she needed her mum to go outside with her.

Juliet got up from the sofa and went with her, while I left them to it and went to the back door to smoke a cigarette while I waited for them to come back indoors. (I don't smoke indoors). A few minutes later Juliet and Victoria walked in through the front door and Juliet called to me. Extinguishing my cigarette, I walked into the kitchen to see Juliet holding a tiny, tan coloured puppy. I was angry of course, and so was Juliet at first as Victoria explained that the puppy, who she'd named Honey, was her Christmas present to her mum. It was obvious that she'd been planning this for some time, as there on the floor in the hall, was a plush dog bed, lead, bowls and toys, including a nice teddy bear, which was as big as the puppy.

The woman who she'd bought the puppy from was the mother of one of her friends and had conspired with her to keep her secret and had just dropped her off outside our house and driven away. Obviously, we were stuck with Honey, and when we got over our initial anger with Victoria, we of course fell for the little baby Juliet held and cuddled in her arms.

Honey!

Victoria told us she was going to pay for the dog's vaccinations and insurance, her food and whatever else she might need, which of course she never did, not that I expected her to. Cute as a button, Honey was a little crossbreed and over the first few weeks, we decided she must have some dachshund in her heritage, as she grew longer and longer without growing taller. As she approaches her second birthday, she hasn't grown much taller, but she is considerably longer! If anyone asks me what breed she is, I jokingly describe her as a 'draught excluder terrier', as she would be great lying across the bottom of a door to keep the draughts out.

As she did with Muffin and Petal, Sasha instantly 'adopted' little Honey, and in the same way, she raised the puppy as if she was Honey's natural mother. Sasha really is quite an incredible dog.

As for Dylan, he as usual accepted the newcomer in our

midst without any fuss at all. When we first placed Honey on the floor to introduce her to the other dogs, he inquisitively sniffed the puppy, and then proceeded to totally ignore her. That was Dylan's way of accepting her, no fuss, no fanfare, just a quick sniff of welcome and then he went about his business as normal.

For the first few weeks of her life with us, Honey slept in her little bed, which we placed in the crate we'd used years ago for Sasha, when she was recuperating from her operations for her broken leg, It was the only way to ensure the other dogs didn't steal and tear up her little teddy. She was a very good puppy and never soiled her crate in the weeks she used it.

Of course, the operative word there was 'puppy' and puppies as you'll all know, love to play. As she grew a bit bigger, more confident and boisterous in her play, Honey tried to get all the dogs in the house to join in her puppy games. Sasha of course was always ready to play with her, and surprisingly, so was Sheba, despite her arthritis.

Once she's had all her vaccinations and was able to join the older dogs on walks, Juliet would take her with any two from Muffin, Digby and Petal, and a set of new play partnerships began with the three of them loving their playtimes with Honey, who loved nothing more than a good old rough and tumble with the 'Honey Monster' as we'd named her.

Honey's big mistake was to try and involve Dylan in her puppy games. It wasn't long before she only had to approach within a few feet of him, and he'd give her the same treatment as Sasha. His screeching bark did the trick and to this day, Honey gives grumpy old Dylan a wide berth.

Poor Dylan, like a lot of elderly people, just can't be doing with the young of today!

Dylan and Penny, OAPs together

Sadly, in June of this year, we had to say goodbye to our dear Dexter, our very special 'bird-dog' who loved being surrounded by the wild birds that visit our garden every day. After a year-long fight against heart and lung problems, he finally left us crossed the Rainbow Bridge. Dylan and Dexter always got on well together and once or twice, I've found Dylan looking around in the garden as if he's searching for his friend.

Rest in Peace, Dexter

16

THE END OF THE BEGINNING

HOW DO I end a story that in reality, shows no sign of ending? Dylan is growing older, but his life is far from over, as he continues to enjoy every day to the full. He still tortures poor Sasha every day by refusing her affectionate advances.

Every morning, as soon as she comes downstairs with us, (She sleeps in our bedroom), she walks into the kitchen and goes around all the dogs, wagging her tail as if to say *Good morning* to each one in turn. As soon as she reaches Dylan, he gives her an earful of his awful screeching bark, telling her to go away. We've pondered long and hard, trying to find a reason for his constant rejection of Sasha, who has never ever done him and harm. In fact, when she was a puppy and for the first two years of her life, he wasn't like this at all with her.

Then, a thought struck both Juliet and I at the same time. Sasha was two and half years old when she had her first epileptic seizure. We know that a couple of our dogs are scared when she goes into a seizure and will try to nip or bite her, and we always move quickly to move them away from her until the seizure is over. We now wondered if perhaps Sasha's scent

ꞏ

changed when she became epileptic and somehow, Dylan could sense she was in some way 'different' and his reaction to her could be connected to this change. We know that a dog's sense of smell is possibly their most important of their senses and its possible that Dylan feels afraid of Sasha because of something her body is giving off in her scent.

This theory is only that, a theory and doesn't explain why he is perfectly normal with her when we're out for a walk together and he walks side by side with Sasha without a problem. Could it be that any sensory change, if that is the reason for his behaviour towards her, is diluted when they're out of doors in the fresh air?

I suppose we'll never know for sure, so Sasha will go on playing the role of star-crossed lover, while Dylan is the grumpy old man, constantly rejecting her advances.

"Who grumpy? Me grumpy? Never!

As for his health issues, we recently learned just how bad his eyesight has become when I took him to the vet for his annual booster injection. I've mentioned previously that Dylan has no problem getting around at home, in the garden or on his regular walks.

When he and I walked into the vet surgery on this occasion, we were greeted warmly by the girls on reception, who are always pleased to see Dylan. As I stood at the desk to check him in, Dylan walked around, to the extent his lead would allow, and bumped into a nearby shelf where bags of specialist dog foods were on display. Next, he bumped into the wall behind the weighing scales when I went to weigh him, and when we were called into the consulting room, he somehow managed to bump himself against the door frame as we walked into the room. The staff in reception were understandably having a laugh at his antics and I told them I thought his blindness was worse, after which they stopped having a laugh and were all sympathetic to little old Dylan.

I mentioned these small incidences to Ximo who examined Dylan's eyes and then advised me that the cataracts were slightly worse, and that Dylan was probably fine at home and in our garden because he knows where everything is. When he arrived at the vets however, he didn't know the layout of the reception area, and probably saw things slightly blurred, hence the reason for him bumping into things.

I felt so sorry for my boy, but Ximo assured me he was fine, just slightly vision impaired, as he put it. As for his walks, he always went on the same two walks and knew the routes by heart and he would have laid his scent trail down many times over the years, so it was fairly easy for him to walk confidently with me, especially as he was on his lead of course. He always keeps very close to Sasha and Sheba as well and I realised one day, he's probably using one or both of them as his personal 'guide dogs', so perhaps he realises that Sasha does have her uses, after all.

As for his hearing, that's another story entirely. As time has passed, Dylan has become harder of hearing month by month. Nowadays, when we're out on our walks and I stop to give the dogs a treat, I always talk to them, usually beginning by saying

"Who wants a biscuit?" and the two staffies immediately sit down in front of me and wait for their treat. Dylan, on the other hand, just stands as if he hasn't heard a word, and when I take the treats from my pocket and reach down to give one to each staffy, and then to Dylan, he doesn't seem to hear me when I say his name and I usually have to give him a little tap to gain his attention and then, when I try to give him his treat, it's as if he can't see it in front of him, and I have to hold it under his nose and let him sniff it until he realises I'm offering him one of his favourite treats. He then takes it slowly from my hand, though sometimes he can't quite see it properly and it falls from his open mouth to the floor, is quickly gobbled up by a staffy and I have to go through the process once again.

Juliet says she doesn't know how I have the patience to go through such a performance just to give him a treat, but I always explain it in the following way.

I have to show incredible patience walking Sasha and Sheba because of their problems, Sasha is often quite slow and makes a lot of stops, because her medications affect her mobility, and Sheba is old and arthritic and can't walk very fast anymore, so I owe it to Dylan to show him the same degree of patience. He's old, can't see very well and doesn't always hear what I'm saying to him, so what if our walk takes an extra five or ten minutes? After all, the walk is primarily for the dog's benefit not ours, so I just allow the old and infirm dogs time to enjoy their walk in their own time. I think they've earned the right to my patience after all these years.

Dylan still loves his food, and unless it's raining, he always has his breakfast and his evening meal outside in the back garden, where he's safe from any of the younger dogs trying to steal his food. He still enjoys his daily denta-stick too, though whether they're doing his teeth any good at this stage in his life is debatable.

"Look, Dad, I made my denta-stick stand up!"

Dylan is and always has been such a lovable boy and having remained fit and healthy for so many years, it's sad to see him growing old and infirm. Having said that, he's still super-fast when he runs, and is happy doing the things he likes, including playtime with his squirrel. He's adjusted well to not being able to see and hear as well as he used to and has already exceeded the average lifespan for a Beddie, that being 12 – 14 years, and we hope he'll have more years ahead of him as the senior member of our rescue pack.

He had a terrible start in life, but he's fought back from those bad times, and though he's undersized, underweight, (compared with an average Bedlington), and occasionally grumpy, we wouldn't have him any other way!

Somehow, life just wouldn't be the same without him.

* * *

Postscript.

Just as I'd finished typing what I thought was the end of Dylan's story, there was a knock at the door. I answered the knocking and found a postman standing on our front step, holding a fairly large parcel, which he handed over to me, and I carried it into the kitchen.

"What's in there?" Juliet asked.

"I've no idea," I replied. "I'm not expecting anything."

Imagine our surprise when, on opening the parcel we found a beautiful padded dog coat and two lovely new dog toys. The enclosed letter was from our friend Kath Bradbury, who had been enormously supportive during our grief after losing Dexter and has been a good friend for some years. Kath owns a lovely Staffy girl, called Poppy who looks very much like our Petal and we laughingly call them 'cousins'.

The letter explained that Kath had bought the coat for Poppy, but it was too big for her, and she thought it might be suitable for one or more of our dogs. The toys were part of a package she'd received, but Poppy isn't allowed soft toys, as she can be destructive with them, so Kath again thought of us.

Doggie presents

One of the toys was a cute dragon, which was just the right size for Dylan to play with, if he'd accept it in lieu of his squirrel. With the other dogs inside the house, I took Dylan into the garden and produced the dragon from behind my back. Dylan immediately began leaping up and down, trying to get the dragon. I threw it, he chased it and picked it up and without any hesitation began tossing it about and shaking it in his mouth, as if it was a rat he'd just caught.

He was so happy, and I spent about ten minutes with him as he played with his new toy. He'd certainly turned the clock back, as the years seemed to fall away as he made that dragon his own and nobody could have guessed that this was a fifteen-year-old dog jumping about like a puppy with his toy.

I'm so grateful to Kath for her thoughtfulness. It appears Dylan's squirrel now has some serious competition in the 'favourite toy' department. To see him jumping and leaping and springing on the dragon, like a spring lamb, was just an amazing sight, and I can safely say, I think that Dylan still has some happy times ahead.

I think it's fitting that I close with these pictures of Dylan and his dragon.

Dylan and 'Dilys' the dragon

DYLAN, Juliet, me and all our family of rescue dogs thank you for reading Dylan's story and hope you've enjoyed this glimpse into his life with us.

Dear reader,

We hope you enjoyed reading *Dylan – The Flying Bedlington*. Please take a moment to leave a review in Amazon, even if it's a short one. Your opinion is important to us.

Discover more books by Brian L Porter at https://www.nextchapter.pub/authors/brian-porter-mystery-author-liverpool-united-kingdom

Want to know when one of our books is free or discounted for Kindle? Join the newsletter at http://eepurl.com/bqqB3H

Best regards,

Brian L Porter and the Next Chapter Team

ABOUT THE AUTHOR

Brian L Porter is an award-winning, bestselling author, whose books have regularly topped the Amazon Best Selling charts. Writing as Brian, he has won a Best Author Award, and his mystery/thrillers have picked up Best Thriller and Best Mystery Awards. The third book in his Mersey Mystery series, *A Mersey Maiden* recently won The Best Book We've Read all Year Award, 2018, from Readfree.ly. In addition, *Cassie's Tale* was the runner-up in the 2018 Top 50 Best Indie Books of the year, at the same time winning the Non-fiction category, and *A Very Mersey Murder* finished in 5th place in the same awards, while also winning the Best Mystery Novel Award. Both *Sasha* and *Sheba: From Hell to Happiness* have won international awards and both books are now international bestsellers.

When it comes to dogs and dog rescue, he is passionate about the subject and his three previous dog rescue books have been hugely successful. Sasha: A Very Special Dog Tale of a Very Special Epi-Dog is now an award-winning international bestseller and Sheba: From Hell to Happiness is also a UK Bestseller and an award winner too. *Cassie's Tale*, the third book in the series, also followed Sasha and Sheba in winning the Critters.org, (formerly Preditors and editors), annual Best Non-fiction award, 2018, and there are sure to be more to follow.

Writing as Harry Porter his children's books have achieved three bestselling rankings on Amazon in the USA and UK.

In addition, his third incarnation as romantic poet Juan Pablo Jalisco has brought international recognition with his collected works, *Of Aztecs and Conquistadors* topping the best-selling charts in the USA, UK and Canada.

Brian lives with his wife, eldest stepdaughter and of course, Sasha and the rest of his wonderful pack of ten rescued dogs, in the North of England.

A Mersey Killing and the subsequent books in his Mersey Mystery series have already been optioned for adaptation as a TV series, in addition to his other novels, all of which have been signed by ThunderBall Films in a movie franchise deal.

The Mersey Mystery Series

OTHER BOOKS BY THE AUTHOR

Dog Rescue Series

Sasha – A Very Special Dog Tale of a Very Special Epi-Dog

Sheba: From Hell to Happiness

Cassie's Tale

Penny the Railway Pup

Remembering Dexter

Thrillers by Brian L Porter

A Study in Red - The Secret Journal of Jack the Ripper

Legacy of the Ripper

Requiem for the Ripper

Pestilence

Purple Death

Behind Closed Doors

Avenue of the Dead

The Nemesis Cell

Kiss of Life

The Mersey Mystery Series

A Mersey Killing (Amazon bestseller)

All Saints, Murder on the Mersey

A Mersey Maiden

A Mersey Mariner

A Very Mersey Murder

Last Train to Lime Street

The Mersey Monastery Murders

(Coming soon) – A Liverpool Lullaby

Short Story Collections

After Armageddon (Amazon bestseller)

Remembrance Poetry

Lest We Forget (Amazon bestseller)

Children's books as Harry Porter

Wolf (Amazon bestseller)

Alistair the Alligator, (Illustrated by Sharon Lewis) (Amazon bestseller)

Charlie the Caterpillar (Illustrated by Bonnie Pelton) (Amazon bestseller)

As Juan Pablo Jalisco

Of Aztecs and Conquistadors (Amazon bestseller)

The award-winning rescue dogs series

Love from all of us

You might also like:

Fully Staffed by Linda A. Meredith

To read the first chapter for free go to:
https://www.nextchapter.pub/books/fully-staffed

Printed in Great Britain
by Amazon